Bankruptcy Law
for the
Individual Debtor

by
Margaret C. Jasper

Oceana's Legal Almanac Series:
Law for the Layperson

1997
Oceana Publications, Inc.
Dobbs Ferry, N.Y.

You may order this or any other Oceana publications by visiting Oceana's Web Site at http://www.oceanalaw.com

Library of Congress Cataloging-in-Publication Data

Jasper, Margaret C.
    Bankruptcy law for the individual debtor / by Margaret C. Jasper.
        p.   cm. -- (Oceana's legal almanac series. Law for the layperson)
    Includes bibliographical references.
    ISBN: 0-379-11240-X (alk. paper)
    1. Bankruptcy--United States--Popular works. I. Title.
II. Series.
KF1524.6.J3 1997
346.7307'8--dc21   97-22513
                                         CIP

Oceana's Legal Almanac Series: Law for the Layperson
ISSN: 1075-7376

Manufactured in the United States of America on acid-free paper.

To My Husband Chris

Your love and support
are my motivation and inspiration

and

In memory of my son, Jimmy

ABOUT THE AUTHOR

MARGARET C. JASPER is an attorney engaged in the general practice of law in South Salem, New York, concentrating in the areas of personal injury and entertainment law. Ms. Jasper holds a Juris Doctor degree from Pace University School of Law, White Plains, New York, is a member of the New York and Connecticut bars, and is certified to practice before the United States District Courts for the Southern and Eastern Districts of New York, and the United States Supreme Court.

Ms. Jasper has been appointed to the panel of arbitrators of the American Arbitration Association and the law guardian panel for the Family Court of the State of New York, and is a New York State licensed real estate broker and member of the Westchester County Board of Realtors, operating as Jasper Real Estate, in South Salem, New York.

Ms. Jasper is the author and general editor of the following legal almanacs: Juvenile Justice and Children's Law; Marriage and Divorce; Estate Planning; The Law of Contracts; The Law of Dispute Resolution; Law for the Small Business Owner; The Law of Personal Injury; Real Estate Law for the Homeowner and Broker; Everyday Legal Forms; Dictionary of Selected Legal Terms; The Law of Medical Malpractice; The Law of Product Liability; The Law of No-Fault Insurance; The Law of Immigration; The Law of Libel and Slander; The Law of Buying and Selling; Elder Law; The Right to Die; AIDS Law; Obscenity, Pornography and the Law; The Law of Child Custody; The Law of Debt Collection; and Consumer Rights Law.

TABLE OF CONTENTS

INTRODUCTION

America is an abundantly wealthy country. Ironically, American economy is largely based on consumer debt. There is a virtually unlimited supply of goods and services, and credit is readily available to those who do not have the cash on hand to make such purchases. The temptation to live beyond one's means is often difficult to resist.

People earnestly try to budget their income to meet all of their obligations. However, a slight disruption of income flow—let alone a major catastrophe, such as a disabling injury or loss of employment—may quickly drive an individual into debt. In some instances, if the debt is not too burdensome, an individual is able to make payment arrangements and manage through the difficult times. Unfortunately, this is often not the case. The debt may be too large to manage, and there may be assets in jeopardy, such as a home or car. The individual may then need to seek judicial protection while trying to manage his or her financial affairs.

This legal almanac explores the law of bankruptcy as it applies to the individual debtor. Bankruptcy is a legal method under federal law by which businesses or individuals resolve or restructure their financial affairs when they are faced with debt problems.

Often an individual may unnecessarily feel guilty over failure to pay his or her debts. Debt collectors attempt to "shame" individuals into making payments they cannot afford. However, creditors expect that a certain number of consumers will at some point be unable to repay their debt, and include this expectation in computing their cost of credit. Consumers often repay their principal debt many times over in finance charges, late payment fees and other costs and assessments. Creditors should bear some responsibility for the aggressive tactics they use in persuading consumers to accumulate debt.

Further, many large companies and financial institutions use the protection afforded under bankruptcy law to solve their financial difficulties. The individual, struggling to support a family, deserves no less protection. This legal almanac is concerned with the remedies available to the individual who is faced with personal indebtedness.

This almanac presents a general discussion of bankruptcy law in the United States, and the bankruptcy court system in operation today. The almanac further discusses the procedure an individual must follow in order to receive the relief sought in his or her bankruptcy petition.

The Appendix provides sample forms, applicable statutes, and other pertinent information and data. The Glossary contains definitions of many of the terms used throughout the almanac.

CHAPTER 1:

MAKING THE DECISION TO FILE BANKRUPTCY

In General

Bankruptcy is designed to give an individual a "fresh start" by discharging, i.e., canceling, certain debts. However, it is important for an individual considering bankruptcy to explore all available alternatives to make sure that there are no less drastic solutions that would solve the individual's financial problems.

This is particularly so when the debtor's liabilities are primarily consumer debt, such as credit card obligations, and the individual is basically "judgment proof"—i.e., he or she has little or no income or assets from which recovery can be made—and no major changes to this scenario are anticipated.

As further discussed below, creditors will usually try to work out a payment arrangement rather than pursue any legal methods of recovering a debt. Often, the cooperative approach is more likely to result in payments being made.

Nevertheless, even if an individual is being harassed by collection agencies, it is still not necessary to immediately file for bankruptcy protection. The consumer is entitled to certain protection under the law to stop debt collection harassment. Debt collectors are legally prohibited from using deceitful or threatening tactics. Further, they are legally prohibited from contacting an individual once they are given written notice that all contact should cease.

A more detailed discussion of debt collection law may be found in this author's legal almanac entitled The Law of Debt Collection (1997), also published by Oceana Publishing Company.

Other than telephoning and writing the debtor to request payment, a creditor has no legal right to collect on a debt unless the creditor sues the debtor and obtains a judgment. Thus, if debt collection efforts fail, a creditor has to make a decision whether it is financially wise to start a lawsuit to recover the debt.

It would be virtually impossible for creditors to sue all of the consumers who fail to pay their debts. The legal fees, costs and the time it takes to obtain a judgment would likely far outweigh any recovery the creditor could expect. Often the creditor will take the uncollected debt and write it off as a cost of doing business—known as a "charge-off"—after a period of time.

Of course, this causes considerable damage to the debtor's credit rating for approximately seven years, but collection action usually ends, and a lawsuit is not likely initiated to recover the debt. Further, once the applicable statute of limitations has expired, the creditor is legally prevented from filing a lawsuit against the debtor.

In considering whether to charge off the debt, or to take legal action, the creditor generally weighs a number of factors, including whether the debtor is judgment proof. If the creditor does decide to sue, and obtains a judgment against the debtor, the creditor must then attempt to collect the judgment amount from the debtor's property and/or income.

There are exemption laws, however, which protect much of the debtor's property from collection. Also, any property which is not protected must be significant for the creditor to pursue collection, because of the attendant costs of seizing and selling the property, e.g. sheriff's poundage charges.

If the creditor places a lien on the debtor's home, unless the lien is in a considerable amount, it is not likely that the creditor will foreclose on the debtor's home to collect the debt. The costs of foreclosure are substantial, and the creditor stands in line behind the mortgage holder, taxing authorities and any previously filed liens before getting paid, if at all. It is more likely that the creditor will wait until the debtor chooses to sell or refinance his or her home, at which time the debt must be paid at or before closing to transfer clear title to the property.

Creditors are more apt to go after a debtor's wages or other income to collect on a judgment. However, public benefits, such as unemployment, public assistance, disability, or social security benefits are generally protected. Also, if there is income—such as wages or pension and retirement benefits—eligible to satisfy a judgment, there are laws which limit the amount that can be taken at any given time.

Thus, consumer debt need not be the catalyst to an immediate bankruptcy filing. If the debtor doesn't have a significant source of steady income, or property which is secured by the debt—e.g. a mortgage or automobile loan—bankruptcy may not be necessary.

Bankruptcy is a serious step which may have certain relatively long-term consequences. One must carefully assess his or her financial situation and determine whether bankruptcy is the right course to take given all of the advantages and disadvantages.

Advantages of Filing Bankruptcy

Legal Protection

Filing bankruptcy gives the debtor some time to rethink his or her financial situation without worrying about a foreclosure sale of his or her home due to mortgage arrears or tax debts. The automatic stay, which is further discussed in Chapter 4, prevents all creditors from taking any legal action against the debtor once the bankruptcy petition has been filed.

Bankruptcy Provides a New Start

According to the National Foundation for Consumer Credit (NFCC), it typically takes three to four years for most individuals who seek NFCC services to repay their accumulated debts. For many others, it takes considerably longer. Credit card debt is particularly difficult to resolve. It is not uncommon for the balance on a credit card account to actually increase despite years of payment and nonuse. This is because the monthly finance charge cancels out a significant portion of the monthly payment, and added late charges may increase the amount owed.

Bankruptcy provides the debtor a legal method to wipe out a significant amount—if not all—of his or her debts. The debtor is given a fresh start to manage his or her financial affairs without this burden. Generally, there is no minimum amount of debt necessary to file for bankruptcy.

Disadvantages of Filing Bankruptcy

Damage to Credit Rating

The most apparent disadvantage of filing for bankruptcy protection is the serious damage inflicted on the debtor's credit rating. A bankruptcy filing can remain on an individual's credit report for 10 years. This generally impedes any efforts to obtain credit, e.g. for a home or automobile purchase, for a considerable period of time.

Nevertheless, an individual who is in debt to the degree that he or she is considering filing bankruptcy has more than likely already sustained considerable damage to his or her credit.

Privacy Factor

Bankruptcy petitions are a matter of public record. The debtor must disclose all of his or her personal financial information for at least the previous two years. All of one's financial dealings are available for public scrutiny.

Unavailability of Subsequent Discharge

Six-Year Restriction

Once a debtor receives a discharge under Chapter 7 or Chapter 13, he or she is ineligible to file for Chapter 7 bankruptcy protection for six years from the date the prior bankruptcy petition was filed. All new debts incurred after the bankruptcy filing must be paid.

Thus, if the individual is faced with a financial crisis within the six-year period, such as loss of employment or a medical emergency, Chapter 7 bankruptcy protection will not be available.

Exceptions to Six-Year Restriction

An exception to the six-year rule exists if the prior discharge was obtained in Chapter 13, in good faith, after the debtor paid at least 70% of his or her unsecured debts.

Further, the six-year rule does not apply if the debtor intends to file Chapter 13 bankruptcy, provided the debtor has enough income to make a plan to repay his or her debts.

180-Day Restriction

Further, an individual is restricted from filing for Chapter 7 bankruptcy if a prior Chapter 7 or Chapter 13 case was dismissed within the previous 180 days (i) due to the debtor's violation of a court order; or (ii) upon the debtor's request after a creditor made a motion for relief from the automatic stay.

Co-signer Liability

Co-signers do not benefit from the discharge obtained by a Chapter 7 debtor. Therefore, if a friend or relative co-signed a loan for you, they will be left wholly responsible for repayment of the debt unless they also file bankruptcy. However, in Chapter 13, the co-signer cannot be pursued for the debt if the debtor agrees to pay the debt in full, remains in Chapter 13, and continues to make payments to the creditor.

CHAPTER 2:

THE BANKRUPTCY SYSTEM

In General

Prior to the enactment of bankruptcy laws, individuals risked being sent to a debtors' prison if they were unable to pay their debts. Failure to pay a debt was looked upon as a very serious offense. This mindset began to change in the late 1800's when laws were enacted to assist persons who found themselves in financial trouble. Although state laws may provide some relief to the debtor, the broadest remedies are found in the federal bankruptcy laws.

Governing Law

Bankruptcy law is governed by the Bankruptcy Code, which was enacted in 1978, with numerous subsequent amendments. The Bankruptcy Code is part of the collection of federal statutes known as the United States Code. The United States Code is broken down into sections known as "Titles." The Bankruptcy Code is Title 11 of the United States Code.

Title 11 is further broken down into sections known as "Chapters" and includes Chapter 7; Chapter 11; Chapter 12; and Chapter 13. The debtor generally chooses which "chapter" of the Bankruptcy Code provides the desired relief, and determines whether he or she is eligible to file under that chapter considering his or her financial circumstances.

This almanac focuses on Chapters 7 and 13, the two chapters which are most applicable to the individual debtor's situation. Chapter 7 bankruptcy involves liquidation of the debtor's assets, and is discussed further in Chapter 6. Chapter 13 of the Bankruptcy Code involves the adjustment of an individual's debt, provided that individual has regular income. The term "income" includes more than one's wages. Chapter 13 bankruptcy is discussed further in Chapter 7.

Chapter 11 of the Bankruptcy Code refers to debt reorganization. Chapter 11 generally involves businesses, but may also apply to certain individuals who do not qualify for Chapter 13 because their unsecured and/or secured debt exceeds the limit provided in the Bankruptcy Code. Chapter 12 of the Bankruptcy Code refers to debt reorganization involving family farmers as defined in the Bankruptcy Code. Chapters 11 and 12 are not discussed in this almanac because they are not generally applicable to the individual debtor.

Before filing for bankruptcy, one must research the law and procedure in his or her own jurisdiction. Bankruptcy law was federally enacted, and was intended to be uniform across the country. However, when conflicts arise in a particular case, a decision is made by the bankruptcy court in which the case is pending.

Unless an appeal is taken to the federal level, or the legislature intervenes to establish a uniform ruling, the various local decisions would be the law in that jurisdiction until statutorily changed or overruled at the appellate level.

In addition, the procedural bankruptcy rules, which are governed by the Federal Rules of Bankruptcy Procedure, are supplemented by the local rules of individual courts.

Therefore, the reader is advised to check the law and practice of their own jurisdiction before filing a bankruptcy petition. Further, if the debtor's financial situation is particularly complex, it is advisable to consult a lawyer before proceeding.

The Bankruptcy Court

The Bankruptcy Court is part of the United States District Court for the district in which the court is located. The bankruptcy court judge presides over all bankruptcy cases. Once a bankruptcy case is filed, it is assigned to a particular bankruptcy court judge, and generally remains with the same judge until its conclusion.

A directory of United States Bankruptcy Courts is set forth in the Appendix.

The United States Trustee

The United States Trustee is an officer of the United States Department of Justice. The U.S. Trustee is responsible for appointing the bankruptcy trustees who oversee the bankruptcy cases pending in the various courts under the U.S. Trustee's jurisdiction.

The Trustee in Bankruptcy

After the bankruptcy petition is filed, a bankruptcy trustee—known as a "trustee in bankruptcy"—is appointed to administer the bankruptcy case and oversee the bankruptcy estate. The bankruptcy trustee acts under the authority of the U.S. Trustee in overseeing the bankruptcy cases pending in a particular court.

Following the filing of the bankruptcy petition, the bankruptcy trustee usually contacts the debtor if additional information is needed, such as copies of tax returns, property appraisals, pension statements, insurance policies, automobile title and registration, deeds, or bank statements.

It is the trustee's obligation to make sure all non-exempt property is uncovered so that the creditors can be paid as much as possible. It is also the trustee's duty to object to inappropriately claimed exemptions, and to object to a debtor's discharge if it is not warranted. In a Chapter 7 case, it is the bankruptcy trustee's duty to gather the debtor's assets and distribute funds to the creditors. In a Chapter 13 case, the bankruptcy trustee's functions are more limited.

The Section 341 Meeting

The bankruptcy trustee reviews the debtor's petition, schedules and all other documentation, and conducts what is known as a Section 341 examination of the debtor. The debtor will be notified of the date and time for the Section 341 meeting, also referred to as the "first meeting of creditors."

The debtor must appear at this meeting or risk having the bankruptcy petition dismissed. If unable to attend on the particular date assigned, the debtor should contact the court for an adjournment.

At the Section 341 meeting, the trustee may ask questions regarding the information contained on the debtor's petition and schedules, including questions concerning the debtor's assets and debts, income and expenses, and employment and household obligations. Examination of the debtor is conducted under oath.

All of the creditors who are listed on the debtor's bankruptcy petition are notified of the date, time and place of the Section 341 meeting. Although the creditors have the right to attend this meeting and question the debtor, they rarely elect to do so in a simple case.

If the trustee is satisfied with the information provided at the meeting, he or she will close the meeting. No further court appearance is generally required after this meeting is closed, although the Bankruptcy Code does permit further examination under §2004 should the need arise.

The Trustee's Avoiding Powers

The bankruptcy trustee has been granted certain rights to negate transactions that the debtor made prior to filing the bankruptcy petition. These rights are known as "avoiding powers." The most common types of transactions which are "avoided" by the trustee are fraudulent conveyances and preferential transfers.

Fraudulent Conveyances

A fraudulent conveyance—also referred to as a fraudulent transfer—involves the disposal of an asset for less than its value. Fraudulent transfers are prohibited under §548 of the Bankruptcy Code. In addition, state statutes also prohibit fraudulent transfers. Many states have adopted either the Uniform Fraudulent Conveyance Act (UFCA) or the Uniform Fraudulent Transfers Act (UFTA) to govern such transfers. The state statutes generally provide a longer period of time during which a pre-petition transfer of property may be deemed fraudulent.

The trustee may deem a transfer fraudulent if: (i) the transfer was made or the obligation incurred during the statutory period; and (ii) the debtor acted with the intent to hinder, delay or defraud the creditors. There are certain criteria the trustee looks for in finding the requisite intent.

These criteria include but are not limited to: (i) whether or not the transferred property was actually transferred; (ii) whether a close relationship existed between the debtor and the person to whom the property was transferred; (iii) whether the debtor received less than full value for the transferred property.

If the debtor received less than full value for the transferred property, additional factors will be necessary to avoid the transfer. For example, it must also be shown that the debtor was insolvent at the time the transfer was made, or that the effect of the transfer was to make the debtor insolvent.

Preferential Transfers

A preferential transfer—commonly referred to simply as a "preference"—is a transfer which is made without any intent to defraud such as that found with fraudulent conveyances. The transfer may include payment on a debt, forgiveness of a debt, or giving a mortgage to a creditor.

In general, a preference involves a transfer by an insolvent person during the preference period, to or for the benefit of a creditor on account of a debt, that gives that creditor more than it would have received in the bankruptcy if the transfer had not been made.

The preference period is generally the ninety-day period prior to the bankruptcy filing. During this time, the debtor is presumed to have been insolvent. If the transfer was made to someone who has a relationship with the debtor, such as a relative or business partner—known as an "insider,"—the preference period is extended for the year prior the bankruptcy filing. However, in that case, the trustee must prove the debtor's insolvency during transfers made prior to the 90-day presumption of insolvency in order to avoid the preference.

Closing the Bankruptcy Case

When all matters relating to the distribution of the estate and the discharge of any debts are concluded, the bankruptcy trustee files the appropriate reports and has the case closed.

CHAPTER 3:

THE BANKRUPTCY PETITION

In General

The bankruptcy petition is a document which sets forth extensive information concerning the debtor and his or her financial situation. The bankruptcy petition is required to be filed in the district where the debtor has resided for the six-month period prior to the filing.

The bankruptcy petition must set forth the debtor's name, address and social security number. If the debtor has ever obtained credit or incurred any debts under another name, that name must also be included in the petition. If a married couple is filing a joint bankruptcy petition, information for both spouses must be set forth on the petition.

A sample bankruptcy petition is set forth in the Appendix.

Schedules

The bankruptcy court is entitled to complete disclosure of all relevant information concerning the debtor. This includes information concerning the debtor's debts and assets; income and expenses; and other information concerning the debtor's financial affairs. This information is included with the bankruptcy petition on official forms known as schedules, as set forth below.

Debts

The debtor must set forth all of his or her liabilities in the bankruptcy petition whether or not the underlying debt is dischargeable. This includes any debts which are disputed or where the amount is uncertain. Each creditor's address must be listed on the petition along with the account number assigned to the particular debt.

It is important that each creditor receive notice that the debtor has filed bankruptcy. Any debt which is not included in the bankruptcy petition might not be discharged unless it is demonstrated that the creditor had actual knowledge of the bankruptcy proceeding and failed to file a proof of claim.

A sample proof of claim is set forth in the Appendix.

Creditors must file their proofs of claim with the bankruptcy court. If they fail to file a claim, they will not be paid. Creditor claims are paid only out of funds that the trustee can obtain from the debtor's non-exempt assets.

Chapter 7 debtors generally have no assets from which to pay creditors. The available exemptions usually exceed their assets and the creditors therefore receive nothing.

Chapter 13 debtors, however, must pay the trustee what their budget demonstrates they can afford under a 3 to 5 year plan. Therefore, Chapter 13 creditors usually receive at least a percentage of their claims.

Bankruptcy debts fall into one of three categories: (i) priority claims; (ii) secured claims; and (iii) unsecured claims.

Priority Claims

In Chapter 7, priority claims are usually first in line to be paid if the debtor has any funds available for distribution to creditors. Full payment of such debts must be contemplated for the Chapter 13 debtor to obtain confirmation of the debtor's Chapter 13 plan.

Priority claims are generally paid in deferred cash payments at various intervals under the plan. Although the Bankruptcy Code does not require that priority claims be paid first, it is advisable to get these claims out of the way before making payments on unsecured debts.

Priority claims would include debts incurred as a result of: (i) Administrative Claims; (ii) Unsecured Tax Claims; and (iii) Wage Claims.

Administrative Claims

Administrative claims are entitled to priority in payment. These include the trustee's commission and expenses.

Unsecured Tax Claims

Income taxes represent the most common type of priority debt for an individual. Taxes which are due for fewer than three years are priority debts which are not dischargeable. Further, if the taxing authority has made a new assessment within eight months of the filing, the tax debt must be listed as a priority and must be paid in full.

Priority tax claims are not allowed post-petition interest, however, interest that accrued prior to the bankruptcy filing must be paid as part of the claim. Pre-petition penalties also become part of the priority tax claim provided they are not punitive in nature. A punitive penalty becomes an unsecured claim in bankruptcy which does not have to be paid in full.

Wage Claims

If the debtor owes wages to an employee for work performed within 90 days prior to the bankruptcy filing, those claims receive priority status in an amount up to the statutorily prescribed limit per individual.

Secured Claims

A secured claim is a debt for which payment is guaranteed by a specific item of property known as collateral. Common types of assets which are generally used as collateral to secure a debt include real property, automobiles, appliances, and jewelry. A secured claim must be paid in full if the debtor wishes to keep the secured asset.

The debtor has the option of surrendering the collateral and giving the creditor an unsecured claim for any deficiency remaining for the difference between the amount of the claim and the value of the surrendered collateral. The debtor may be able to modify the terms and interest rate of secured claims with the exception of a secured claim for the debtor's principal residence.

The most common type of secured debt is a homeowner's mortgage. If the homeowner does not pay the mortgage payments, the lender has the contractual right to foreclose on the property. In general, if a Chapter 13 debtor wants to keep his or her home, the original loan must be reinstated by paying the mortgage arrears, and maintaining the payments under the original loan terms during the life of the plan and thereafter.

Under a Chapter 13 plan, a secured creditor retains their lien on the secured property, and must receive payments under the plan that equal the present value of the asset securing the claim. The secured creditor is also entitled to be compensated for depreciation.

Unsecured Claims

Unsecured claims represent the majority of debts listed by an individual debtor. The most common types of unsecured claims include: (i) credit card debt; (ii) medical and hospital bills; (iii) utility bills; (iv) rent; (v) non-priority taxes; (vi) student loans; (vii) deficiency claims; and (viii) personal loans.

Under the Bankruptcy Code, unsecured claims may be classified differently according to how similar they are to each other. However, this doesn't mean that one class can be given any preferential treatment over another class in terms of payment. For example, you can't pay seventy-five percent of a credit card company's unsecured claim, but pay only fifty percent of a hospital's unsecured claim. All unsecured creditors must receive the same percentage of payment.

Further, each unsecured creditor must receive no less than what it would receive if the debtor filed under Chapter 7 and liquidated some or all of the property of the estate.

Assets

The debtor must set forth all of his or her assets in the bankruptcy petition. There must be full disclosure of each item of property owned by the debtor, or in which the debtor had an interest, as of the date the bankruptcy petition is filed. These assets may include but are not limited to the following:

1. Real property, including homes, coops, condos, time-shares, gravesites and investment property;

2. Bank accounts, safe deposit boxes and cash on hand;

3. Household goods such as furniture, televisions, stereos, and computers;

4. Books, art and collectibles;

5. Jewelry, clothing and other personal possessions;

6. Motor vehicles, including cars, trucks, mobile homes, and motorcycles;

7. Boats and boating equipment;

8. Business assets such as office furniture and machinery; patents and copyrights;

9. Interests in insurance policies, wills, trusts, pensions, profit sharing, annuities, IRAS, Keogh and retirement plans;

10. Interests in legal actions the debtor has against another;

11. Tax refunds.

Income and Expenses

The debtor must set forth in the bankruptcy petition a detailed list of his or her budget, including current sources of income and regular expenses. Income includes wages, commissions, business income, investment income, tax refunds, rental income, public benefits, unemployment compensation, etc. The expenses should be listed as they will exist after the bankruptcy petition is filed.

The bankruptcy judge will use this information to determine whether the debtor can repay his or her creditors without bankruptcy protection. If so, the case may be dismissed.

In Chapter 13, the amount the debtor will have to pay monthly according to his or her repayment plan will be based on the budget presented to the court. Any changes in the debtor's income or expenses during the bankruptcy proceeding should be disclosed to the court.

Statement of Affairs

Another important schedule which makes up the bankruptcy petition is the debtor's Statement of Affairs. The Statement of Affairs includes information about the debtor's financial affairs which may not be apparent in the other schedules. The Statement of Affairs includes information such as:

1. All names the debtor has used or been known by in the previous six years.

2. The debtor's current address and former addresses for the previous six years.

3. The debtor's current place of employment, occupation and income for the previous two years.

4. Names of partnerships or other businesses the debtor has engaged in within the previous six years.

5. Tax refunds due the debtor or which were received by the debtor in the previous two years.

6. Information concerning the debtor's safe deposit boxes, if any.

7. Information concerning the debtor's bank accounts, credit union accounts, brokerage accounts and/or pension funds.

8. Information concerning the debtor's financial books and records, if any.

9. Information concerning property the debtor is holding for another party and/or property being held by another party for the debtor.

10. Information concerning any prior bankruptcy filings by the debtor.

11. Information concerning any lawsuits, garnishments or property seizures pending against the debtor.

12. Information concerning all payments made to creditors within the previous year.

13. Information concerning the transfer of property or gifts from the debtor to relatives within the previous year.

14. Information concerning repossessions, casualty losses or gambling losses within the previous year.

15. Information concerning payment and/or payment agreements with attorneys and/or budget or credit counseling services.

Statement of Intention

A Statement of Intention is a schedule filed in a Chapter 7 case which provides the court with information concerning the debtor's intentions relating to assets which secure debts, such as the debtor's home or car. The debtor must disclose whether he or she intends to retain the asset or surrender it.

If the debtor wishes to keep the asset, he or she must continue to pay for it. An agreement may be reached with the creditor for payment. This agreement must be in writing and may require approval by the bankruptcy judge. The debtor generally has two options for payment of the debt: (i) Reaffirmation; and (ii) Redemption.

Reaffirmation

The debtor may reaffirm the debt by agreeing to continue payments until the debt has been paid in full. Reaffirmations must be made within forty-five days of filing the bankruptcy petition. If the debtor reaffirms the debt, he or she may rescind the reaffirmation within sixty days after the agreement is filed with the court, or at any time prior to discharge, whichever occurs later.

Redemption

An alternative to reaffirmation is redemption. Redemption must take place within forty-five days of filing the bankruptcy petition. The debtor may redeem certain property by agreeing to pay the creditor the full current value of the property in one lump sum, even if the debt is considerably higher.

Property which may be redeemed generally includes tangible personal property intended for personal, family or household use, on which a lien has been filed. In addition, if the bankruptcy trustee abandons a piece of property from the bankruptcy estate, the debtor generally has the right to redeem that property as well.

Declarations

The bankruptcy petition includes declarations which must be signed by the debtor attesting to the accuracy of the information contained in the petition. Therefore, it is important that the information set forth in the bankruptcy petition be accurate. If false or incorrect information is listed, it can jeopardize the debtor's case. The debtor is advised to carefully read the entire petition before signing the declarations.

Filing the Petition

A bankruptcy case is started with the filing of the completed bankruptcy petition and the appropriate filing fee. The debtor may be able to pay the filing fee in installments over a specified period of time, provided it is paid in full prior to the discharge of debts. If a Chapter 7 debtor's financial situation is particularly poor, he or she may apply to the court to have the filing fee waived.

A sample application and order to pay the filing fee in installments is set forth in the Appendix.

The debtor should always keep copies of all of the documents filed with the court. Generally, the petition must be filed in the district where the debtor maintains his or her residence. The bankruptcy court will send the debtor a notice which contains important information concerning the bankruptcy case. This information may include:

1. The bankruptcy case number.

2. The date the petition was accepted for filing.

3. The name of the bankruptcy judge assigned to the case.

4. The name of the bankruptcy trustee assigned to the case.

5. The date, time and place of the debtor's examination by the trustee.

6. A statement regarding the automatic stay provision.

7. Information concerning when and how creditors must file their claims.

8. The date by which objections to discharge must be filed.

9. For Chapter 13 debtors, the details of the plan requirements to repay creditors.

Involuntary Petitions

Creditors can petition the bankruptcy court to have an individual debtor placed into bankruptcy involuntarily under Chapter 7. Involuntary petitions are not accepted under Chapter 13. Involuntary petitions generally require a certain number of creditors to sign the bankruptcy petition depending on the total number of creditors, and the total dollar amount of the claims. If an individual debtor is faced with an involuntary bankruptcy petition, he or she is advised to consult an attorney.

A sample summons served on a debtor in an involuntary bankruptcy case is set forth in the Appenidix.

Executory Contracts

Executory contracts are agreements which have not been fully completed at the time the debtor files his or her bankruptcy petition. Executory contracts may include residential leases; automobile leases; equipment leases; employment agreements; home improvement contracts; and contracts for the future delivery of goods or services.

The most common type of executory contract in an individual bankruptcy is a lease, which is also deemed property of the estate. A Chapter 13 debtor may choose to either terminate or assume an executory contract at any time prior to plan confirmation by the court.

A Chapter 7 debtor must disclose his or her intention regarding executory contracts in the bankruptcy petition. The Chapter 7 trustee has 60 days after the entry of the order for relief to assume or reject a residential or personal property lease. An extension of time may be granted upon application to the bankruptcy judge.

Because a lease is property of the estate, if it has value, a Chapter 7 trustee may assume the lease so it can be sold to a third party and provide proceeds from which to pay creditors. If the lease has no value, the trustee will likely reject it. If no action is taken within the applicable time period, or any extensions thereof, the lease is considered abandoned by the trustee and deemed rejected.

If a lease—or other executory contract—is rejected, the non-bankruptcy party to the lease is given a general unsecured claim for any damages suffered as a result of the rejection. However, there are statutory limits on the damages which may be claimed.

Adversary Proceedings

If a creditor wishes to challenge the discharge of a specific debt, the creditor must begin an adversary proceeding within the bankruptcy case and serve these papers upon the debtor. A creditor may choose to challenge a discharge if, for example, the creditor believes that the debtor committed some wrongful act, such as fraud.

The adversary proceeding must be started within 60 days after the date set for the first meeting of creditors. The debtor must respond if he or she wishes to oppose the creditor's action.

In addition, there are certain types of debts which will not be discharged unless the debtor starts his or her own adversary proceeding. These include debts such as student loans and taxes.

CHAPTER 4:

THE AUTOMATIC STAY

In General

Upon filing the bankruptcy petition with the Bankruptcy Court Clerk, the debtor is afforded certain protections. The most significant of these protections is the automatic stay. The automatic stay prevents the debtor's creditors from taking any further action to collect debts. Anyone who violates the automatic stay by continuing to pursue legal action may be held in contempt of court and suffer penalties as a result.

A sample order restraining creditors pursuant to the automatic stay is set forth in the Appendix.

Section 362 of the Bankruptcy Code details the provisions of the automatic stay. Its major provisions are discussed below.

Suspension of Legal Action

In general, the automatic stay suspends the following types of action:

1. Wage garnishment;

2. Foreclosure;

3. Eviction or utility service suspension;

4. Automobile repossession; and

5. Lawsuits which are pending or which could have been filed prior to the bankruptcy filing, which are based upon failure to pay a debt.

The complete text of Section 362 of the Bankruptcy Code is set forth in the Appendix

The purpose of the automatic stay is to take some of the pressure off of the debtor by allowing him or her to work within the bankruptcy system to manage their financial debt, without having to simultaneously deal with creditors. In order to fully take advantage of the automatic stay, the debtor should immediately notify all of his or her creditors instead of waiting for the court to make the notification.

Exceptions to the Automatic Stay

There are certain exceptions to the automatic stay that have been put into place by legislation and/or the judiciary. Examples of such exceptions include but are not limited to the following:

1. The commencement or continuation of criminal proceedings against the debtor are not subject to the stay. In criminal proceedings that involve both a crime and a debt, the automatic stay will only serve to suspend that portion of the proceedings that involves payment of the debt. For example, if an individual is convicted of criminal mischief for breaking a window, and is sentenced to fifteen days in jail and restitution for the cost of the window, a bankruptcy filing may stay payment of the restitution amount, but won't affect the incarceration.

2. The commencement or continuation of collection actions for alimony, maintenance or support, from property that is not property of the bankruptcy estate, are not subject to the stay. Further, paternity actions and lawsuits seeking to establish, modify or enforce child support or alimony, are not stayed by a bankruptcy filing.

3. Taxing authorities may be stayed from filing a tax lien or seizing the debtor's property, however, they may continue to conduct audits, demand tax returns, and issue tax assessments and demands for payment of the assessed tax.

4. The commencement or enforcement of any action by a governmental unit under its police powers which generally concerns public health and safety, and environmental and related matters, is not subject to the stay.

5. If a lease or other tenancy for nonresidential real estate was terminated by the landlord prior to the bankruptcy filing, the landlord may continue to enforce its rights to obtain possession despite the stay.

Lifting the Automatic Stay

Unless the action falls under an exception as set forth above, a creditor must make a motion to the bankruptcy court to lift—i.e., remove—the stay as it pertains to that creditor. A hearing will be held at which time the creditor must demonstrate to the court that the stay is not serving its intended purpose.

For example, a debtor may file for bankruptcy protection to stop the foreclosure on his or her house. However, if it is determined that the debtor has no equity in the house—i.e., the amount of debt exceeds the fair market value of the house—and no way of repaying the arrears on the mortgage, the court may grant the mortgage holder's motion to lift the automatic stay. This enables the secured creditor to proceed with the foreclosure and sale of the property.

Effect of Property Abandonment on the Automatic Stay

If the bankruptcy trustee who is administering the bankruptcy estate believes that there is no equity in certain property of the estate, the trustee may "abandon" the property. That is because the trustee's duty is to sell assets in order to create a fund from which creditors will be repaid. A piece of property in which the debtor has no equity will add nothing to this fund.

When a particular piece of property is abandoned by the trustee, it reverts to the debtor, at which time the holders of mortgages and liens are free to proceed against it. It is no longer protected under the automatic stay.

CHAPTER 5:

PROPERTY OF THE BANKRUPTCY ESTATE

In General

When anticipating bankruptcy, an individual is always concerned about what property he or she will be able to keep, and what property he or she will have to give up in exchange for the cancellation of debts. Many people mistakenly fear that they will be left with "nothing but the clothes on their back."

This is an incorrect assumption. As set forth below, the law permits the debtor to protect certain property from creditors even if the value of the debtor's assets is greater than his or her debts. These items are known as "exempt property" and they are not included in the debtor's assets available for distribution to creditors.

The Bankruptcy Estate

The filing of a bankruptcy petition creates what is known as a "bankruptcy estate" and the debtor's financial affairs are placed under the legal control of the trustee of the bankruptcy estate. The bankruptcy estate includes all legal or equitable interests the debtor may have in any item of property as of the date the petition is filed.

In addition, property which is obtained after the petition is filed may be included as property of the bankruptcy estate if it falls into the following categories:

1. Inherited property which the debtor has a right to receive within 180 days of the bankruptcy filing;

2. Divorce settlement property which the debtor has a right to receive within 180 days of the bankruptcy filing;

3. Life insurance proceeds which the debtor has a right to receive within 180 days of the bankruptcy filing;

4. Recoveries made by the bankruptcy trustee in avoiding fraudulent transfers and sales;

5. Community property owned by a married couple which is under the sole, equal or joint control of the spouse who filed bankruptcy may be included; and

6. Certain other types of property interests that the bankruptcy estate obtains after the bankruptcy filing.

The debtor is not legally permitted to sell any of the property which is deemed part of the bankruptcy estate. However, the debtor generally remains in control of his or her exempt property, and property the debtor acquires after the petition was filed.

Exemptions

It is important for the debtor to carefully review his or her assets before filing the petition, and compare them to the list of exemptions permitted in the debtor's jurisdiction. If the debtor does not claim an exemption to which he or she may be entitled, the property may be lost. Any property which is not protected by an exemption may be sold by the bankruptcy trustee, and the proceeds used to satisfy creditor claims.

Federal Exemptions

Section 522(d) of the Bankruptcy Code specifies the items of personal and real property which a creditor cannot take to satisfy a claim. These items are known as the federal bankruptcy exemptions.

A list of the federal Bankruptcy Code exemptions under §522(d) is set forth in the Appendix.

Federal Bankruptcy Code exemptions under §522(d) are only available in Connecticut, District of Columbia, Hawaii, Massachusetts, Michigan, Minnesota, Mississippi, New Jersey, New Mexico, Pennsylvania, Rhode Island, Texas, Vermont, Washington, Wisconsin.

In those states, a debtor may choose to take either (i) the §522(d) exemptions, or (ii) the applicable state exemptions combined with any applicable federal exemptions other than those found in Bankruptcy Code §522(d). However, the debtor cannot pick and choose exemptions from amongst the two categories.

State Exemptions

All other states have "opted out" of the federal Bankruptcy Code exemptions under §522(d). These states require their debtors in bankruptcy to exempt property solely according to the applicable state law combined with any applicable federal exemptions other than those found in §522(d) of the Bankruptcy Code.

A list of non-bankruptcy federal exemptions is set forth in the Appendix.

Property generally deemed exempt under most state statutes includes but is not limited to the following:

1. A homestead exemption which exempts part of the equity you have in your home;

2. Motor vehicles up to a certain amount;

3. Clothing and household goods and furnishings which are reasonably necessary;

4. Household appliances;

5. Jewelry up to a certain amount, and personal effects;

6. Life insurance up to a certain amount;

7. A portion of the debtor's earned but yet unpaid wages;

8. Pensions;

9. Tools of the debtor's trade or profession up to a certain amount; and

10. Public benefits such as unemployment, public assistance, disability and social security benefits.

A table of state statutes governing bankruptcy exemptions is set forth in the Appendix.

Objections

The bankruptcy trustee and creditors are entitled to file objections to the debtor's list of exempt property. Objections must be filed within thirty days after the Section 341 meeting unless the court grants an extension of time. The court will determine whether the objections have any merit.

CHAPTER 6:

CHAPTER 7 BANKRUPTCY CASE

In General

Chapter 7 bankruptcy is generally applicable to the individual debtor who has a considerable amount of debt and limited assets.

Discharge of Debts

Chapter 7 bankruptcy—also known as "straight" bankruptcy—serves to cancel out, i.e. discharge, most of the debtor's debts. Such debts generally include credit card debt, medical and hospital bills, and other dischargeable debts.

The bankruptcy trustee or a creditor can file a complaint and claim that there are reasons that the discharge should be denied, e.g. the debts were incurred involving larceny, fraud, and embezzlement. The filing of such a complaint is known as the commencement of an "adversary proceeding," and is discussed further in Chapter 3.

If there are no complaints filed which object to the discharge, the law provides that a discharge order must issue upon expiration of the time for filing objections—60 days following the Section 341 meeting. After the debtor takes the allowable deductions, creditors are paid from the sale of the debtor's remaining assets, if any.

Obtaining a discharge means that the creditor to whom the debt was owed can no longer make any efforts to collect on the discharged debt. If a duly notified creditor takes action to collect on a discharged debt, the creditor may be held in contempt of court. This is so even if the creditor had previously obtained a judgment against the debtor prior to the bankruptcy filing.

Non-Dischargeable Debts

In a Chapter 7 case, certain debts will not be discharged even if they are listed on the debtor's bankruptcy petition. A non-dischargeable debt must be paid regardless of the bankruptcy filing. Non-dischargeable debts may include:

1. Taxes and tax penalties for each of the previous three years. A tax claim for a tax return which was not filed or was filed fraudulently, will not be discharged. If the tax return was filed late, it will not be dischargeable within two years after the return was filed. Further, if there is a new assessment of the tax—e.g., an IRS determination that additional taxes

are owed—it will not be dischargeable if the petition is filed within 240 days of the new assessment.

2. A debt obtained by fraud, false pretenses, a false representation or a false written statement regarding the debtor's financial condition is not dischargeable. For example, if the debtor applied for a loan and intentionally failed to disclose the extent of his or her other liabilities, and was thus granted credit, that debt may not be discharged. In this case, the creditor making such an allegation must take action within 60 days of the first meeting of creditors by commencing an adversary proceeding.

3. Debts for certain luxury purchases or cash advances which exceed a certain dollar amount, and which are made within 60 days before the bankruptcy petition is filed, may not be discharged. In this case, the creditor making such an allegation must take action within 60 days of the first meeting of creditors by commencing an adversary proceeding.

4. A debt which is not listed on the debtor's bankruptcy petition is not dischargeable unless it is demonstrated that the creditor received actual notice that the debtor filed bankruptcy.

5. Debts resulting from embezzlement, larceny or fraud committed by the debtor while acting in a fiduciary capacity may not be discharged.

6. Alimony, separate maintenance and child support may not be discharged.

7. Fines and penalties assessed by a governmental agency, such as parking tickets, may not be discharged.

8. Student loans may not be discharged. However, a loan due for less than seven years may be dischargeable if the debtor can show that repayment would impose a severe financial hardship. Nevertheless, the debtor would have to show that it would be impossible to make even the smallest payments, and that the debtor had made good faith payment efforts in the past.

9. A debt arising from the debtor's driving while under the influence of alcohol or drugs may not be discharged.

10. A debt for restitution included in the debtor's conviction of a crime, and/or criminal fines, may not be discharged.

Certain debts that may not be dischargeable under Chapter 7, may be dischargeable under Chapter 13. If the debtor's financial situation includes mortgage or rent arrears, back taxes or other secured debt, or if the debtor has substantial assets, Chapter 13 may provide the better alternative.

Denial of Discharge

The issuance of a discharge in bankruptcy is usually automatic. Nevertheless, the bankruptcy court may deny a discharge in the following instances:

1. The filing fee was not paid in full.

2. The debtor failed to comply with orders of the trustee or bankruptcy judge.

3. The debtor received a bankruptcy discharge in the last six years.

4. The debtor concealed, destroyed or transferred property with the intent to hinder, delay or defraud, within one year before the bankruptcy petition was filed, or after its filing.

5. The debtor intentionally concealed or destroyed records of his or her financial dealings unless it can be shown that there was a good reason for doing so.

6. The debtor lied under oath at the first meeting of creditors or at any other bankruptcy court hearing.

7. The debtor failed to adequately explain the loss of assets.

The discharge applies to the debtor alone. Any co-signers or guarantors will still be liable to the creditor for any discharged debts unless the debtor agreed to pay the debt in full. In addition, if one spouse files for bankruptcy and the other does not, the non-filing spouse is still liable for any joint debts.

Conversion

If the bankruptcy judge determines that the debtor has enough assets or income to repay his or her debts over a three to five year period, the judge may convert the Chapter 7 case into a Chapter 13 case. Some of the factors considered include:

1. The nature of the debt. For example, if a considerable amount of the debt is consumer debt, this would weigh in favor of conversion.

2. The debtor's property and income. If the debtor has adequate income and/or substantial property, this would weigh in favor of conversion.

Closing the Chapter 7 Case

In a Chapter 7 case, the debtor must surrender all of his or her non-exempt property to the trustee. The property is subsequently sold so that a pool of money is made available from which to pay the creditors.

There are a number of methods in which a debtor surrenders his or her property. For example, the debtor may turn the property over to the trustee, or may pay the trustee the fair market value of the property. If the property is insignificant, the trustee may "abandon" the property, in which case it reverts to the debtor.

Prior to closing the case, the assets are distributed. After the secured creditors are paid, the remaining assets are sold and the proceeds are distributed to the creditors. Generally, payment is made in the following order:

1. Administration expenses and fees;

2. Certain claims in involuntary cases;

3. Unpaid wages, salaries and commissions due to employees and certain independent sales persons which were earned within 90 days of the bankruptcy filing up to the statutorily specified amount per individual;

4. Contributions to employee benefit plans within specified limits;

5 Certain claims of farmers and fishermen up to the statutorily specified amount per claim;

6. Consumer deposits up to the statutorily specified amount per person;

7. Alimony, maintenance and support obligations;

8. Unsecured tax claims; and

9. General creditors.

After distribution to the creditors has taken place, the debtor receives a discharge from all liabilities except for those determined to be nondischargeable or those which have been reaffirmed. Once this discharge has been obtained, the Chapter 7 case is closed.

CHAPTER 7:

CHAPTER 13 BANKRUPTCY CASE

In General

Unlike Chapter 7, which calls for liquidation of the debtor's debts, and the surrender and sale of nonexempt property, a Chapter 13 bankruptcy is designed to reorganize the debtor's financial situation.

The typical Chapter 13 debtor files for bankruptcy protection because he or she: (i) is in arrears with mortgage payments, rent, automobile notes or other secured debt; (ii) has a considerable amount of debt which is not dischargeable in a Chapter 7 proceeding; and/or (iii) has assets which do not qualify as exemptions.

Eligibility

In order to qualify for Chapter 13, the debtor must be an individual with regular income. Income is not limited to wages, but includes and is not limited to earnings derived from sources such as: (i) social security; (ii) unemployment; (iii) alimony and child support; (iv) public assistance benefits; (v) commissions; (vi) rents; (vii) pensions; and (viii) any other type of income which can be estimated.

In addition, the individual's debts cannot exceed $750,000 in secured debt and $250,000 in unsecured debt. If so, the debtor may reorganize his or her debts pursuant to Chapter 11 of the Bankruptcy Code. Because Chapter 11 generally deals with businesses, it is not covered in this almanac.

Businesses are not eligible to file Chapter 13 bankruptcy even if the business is a sole proprietorship. However, if the individual debtor is the owner of a business—excluding stockbrokers and commodity brokers—the debtor may include business-related debts in his or her Chapter 13 case, provided the debtor is personally liable for such debts.

A family farmer is not eligible to file Chapter 13 bankruptcy. A family farmer must file for reorganization pursuant to Chapter 12 of the Bankruptcy Code, which is not covered in this almanac.

The Plan

In Chapter 13, an individual may be able to discharge most of his or her debts by paying all or a portion of them over a three-to-five year period under a repayment plan. The 3-year period is the longest provided for unless the debtor obtains permission from the court, for good cause, to extend the payment plan up to the full five years.

The plan generally includes information concerning the manner in which the debtor intends to comply with the terms of the plan. For example, the plan includes the amount of payments the debtor will contribute to the plan fund, the source of those payments, and the intervals at which the payments will be made, e.g. monthly.

The plan further describes the claims to be paid, which information should be consistent with the debtor's bankruptcy petition. The debtor must provide for the payment of priority claims, setting forth the amounts and a schedule by which the priority claims will be paid in full, unless the holder of the claim agrees otherwise. A classification of unsecured claims must also be included in the plan, setting forth the percentage or amount that the unsecured creditors will be paid under the plan.

If the debtor hired an attorney, the legal fee to be paid should be set forth in the plan. If the debtor intends to surrender property to fund the plan, or make payments outside the plan, a statement as to those intentions should be included, as well as a provision concerning payment of the debtor's post-petition claims.

The Chapter 13 plan must be filed either with the bankruptcy petition or within fifteen days after filing. Payments under the plan generally begin within thirty days of filing. If the debtor begins making these payments, it demonstrates to the trustee, the debtor's ability to comply with the plan, and facilitates confirmation.

A Chapter 13 plan may be modified at any time prior to confirmation without court order, however, the modified plan must comply with all applicable bankruptcy provisions. Creditors whose rights will be negatively affected by the modification are entitled to notice and the opportunity to accept or reject the modified plan.

Unlike Chapter 7, the debtor's nonexempt property is not sold to pay creditors. The Chapter 13 debtor uses his or her future income to make the payments under the debtor's proposed plan.

In general, the debtor must show that he or she has enough income to pay for his or her necessities, and the necessities of the debtor's dependents, and still have enough money remaining to make payments under the plan. This is referred to as the debtor's disposable income. The payments the debtor must make depend on a number of factors, including the amount of debt, and the nature of the debts, e.g. whether they are required to be paid in full.

Taxing authorities are first in line to be paid. Following in line for payment would be mortgage holders, landlords and other secured creditors. These creditors must be paid in full over the three-to-five year period under the plan if the debtor wants to keep the asset which secures the debt. After the foregoing creditors are paid, the unsecured creditors receive the remainder, and are not necessarily paid in full.

If a Chapter 13 debtor becomes unable to make the payments under the plan—e.g. due to illness or loss of employment—the bankruptcy trustee may assist the debtor in modifying the repayment plan. The main concern is that the debtor make a good faith effort to comply. In extreme cases, where it is unlikely that the debtor will be able to continue making payments, the debtor may be able to claim hardship and acquire a discharge of the debts.

The Confirmation Hearing

At some point after the Section 341 Meeting is held by the bankruptcy trustee, a plan confirmation hearing will be scheduled. All of the parties are entitled to copies of the debtor's repayment plan, as well as notice of the time, date and location of the plan confirmation hearing.

Objections

Any party has the right to file an objection to the debtor's repayment plan. The objection must be filed with the court and a copy sent to the debtor. The debtor must respond to any objections filed with the court.

At the confirmation hearing, the bankruptcy judge will rule on any objections raised by creditors or the bankruptcy trustee. The court cannot confirm the debtor's repayment plan over an objection by an unsecured creditor unless it makes a finding that (i) the value of the property being distributed under the plan will pay the claim of the objecting party in full; or (ii) the debtor proposes to pay into the plan all of his or her disposable income for three years beginning on the date the first payment under the plan is due.

Criteria for Confirmation

Even if there are no objections, the court cannot confirm a debtor's repayment plan unless it meets with the Bankruptcy Code's criteria for confirmation, as follows:

1. The debtor's plan must comply with all of the provisions of Chapter 13 and all other applicable provisions of the Bankruptcy Code.

2. The debtor must have paid the filing fee—unless the court at its discretion confirms the plan and permits the debtor to pay the filing fee in in-

stallments—and any other administrative or court fees, or required deposits pursuant to the plan.

3. The debtor's plan must have been proposed in good faith and not in any manner forbidden by law.

4. The debtor's plan must satisfy the "best interests of the creditors' test. In order to satisfy this test, the court must find that the payments made under the plan to unsecured creditors is not less than the amount of money that they would receive if the Chapter 13 case were converted to a Chapter 7. This test protects the unsecured creditors who are not permitted to vote on accepting or rejecting the plan.

5. If the debtor's plan does not provide for the payment of secured claims, those creditors my move for relief from the automatic stay so that they can enforce their rights. However, if the plan does provide for payment of secured claims, one of the following criteria must be met in order for the plan to be confirmed: (i) the secured creditors must accept—or fail to object to—the plan; or (ii) the plan must provide that the secured creditors retain their liens or receive the value of their allowed secured claims on the effective date of the plan; or (iii) the debtor must surrender the property securing the claim to the secured creditor.

6. The court must find that the plan is feasible, i.e., that the debtor will be able to comply with the terms of the plan.

Effect of Confirmation

Confirmation of the debtor's plan obligates both the debtor and the creditors. The debtor most comply with the terms of the plan and the creditors are bound to accept those terms, even if they previously objected to or rejected the plan. Further, creditors who failed to object are similarly bound.

Creditors are forbidden to collect on their debts following confirmation. However, if the debtor fails to make the payments called for in the plan, a creditor may make a motion to the court to lift the automatic stay due to the debtor's noncompliance with the plan.

In addition, confirmation of the debtor's plan vests all of the property of the debtor's bankruptcy estate in the debtor. The property is no longer encumbered by creditors' claims except for secured creditors who are covered by the plan and entitled to maintain their liens.

Post-Confirmation Matters

Payments Under the Plan

Under the plan, the debtor is placed on a strict budget. He or she makes monthly payments to the bankruptcy trustee, who distributes the income amongst the creditors according to the terms of the plan. As set forth below, if the court or the trustee determines that the debtor does not have enough disposable income to fund the monthly budget, the Chapter 13 case may be dismissed or converted to a Chapter 7 case.

Modification of the Plan

Circumstances may arise which were not expected at the time the original plan was confirmed, which may call for modification of the debtor's plan. For example, the plan may be modified to increase or decrease the amounts of payments, or to lengthen or shorten the time the debtor has to make such payments.

A plan modification may be requested by the debtor, the bankruptcy trustee, or an unsecured creditor. A hearing is required on notice to all parties who will be affected by the modification. In order for the court to grant a modification, the modified plan must meet all of the requirements of the original plan, as set forth above.

Conversion

If the court will not grant the debtor a hardship discharge, the debtor may be able to convert the Chapter 13 case to a Chapter 7 case, and seek discharge of the debts under Chapter 7 provisions. However, if the debtor has had a Chapter 7 discharge within the previous six years, conversion is not permitted.

A motion to convert a case from Chapter 13 to Chapter 7 may also be initiated by the bankruptcy trustee or a creditor. Before this occurs, there must be a hearing upon notice to all of the creditors. The creditors have the right to object to the motion.

If the debtor's plan is converted to Chapter 7, the conversion operates to vacate any confirmation order. Debts incurred after filing the plan will be treated as pre-petition claims and discharged in the Chapter 7 case, provided they were incurred prior to the conversion.

There is some conflict amongst the jurisdictions as to whether property acquired after the Chapter 13 case was filed becomes property of the bankruptcy estate. The reader is advised the check the law of his or her own jurisdiction to determine how such property is treated.

Dismissal

If it is deemed that the debtor no longer needs Chapter 13 bankruptcy protection, the case can be dismissed. The debtor can request a dismissal, or a motion to dismiss the case may be brought by the bankruptcy trustee or a creditor upon notice to all creditors. Dismissal of a Chapter 13 case also requires a hearing and the creditors are entitled to object to the dismissal.

If the Chapter 13 case is dismissed, the debtor does not receive a discharge of debts. Further, the dismissal may negate certain other actions taken during bankruptcy. However, the court will not reverse the authorized good faith sale of property. Unless the 180-day restriction discussed in Chapter 1 applies, the debtor is generally able to refile for bankruptcy at any time.

Criteria for Conversion or Dismissal

The Bankruptcy Code sets forth certain criteria which may be grounds for the conversion or dismissal of a Chapter 13 case, including:

1. An unreasonable delay that prejudices the creditors;

2. The debtor's nonpayment of fees and charges;

3. The debtor's failure to timely file a plan;

4. The debtor's failure to commence making payments under the plan within thirty days of its filing;

5. The court's denial of confirmation and denial of the debtor's request for additional time in which to file an alternate plan;

6. A material default concerning the terms of the confirmed plan;

7. A revocation of the order which confirmed the debtor's plan, and denial of confirmation of a modified plan.;

8. Termination of a confirmed plan by reason of an occurrence which is specified in the plan, other than completion of the payments under the plan;

9. Failure of the debtor to file a list of creditors, schedules, and a statement of financial affairs.

Discharge

Full Compliance Discharge

When all of the payments under the plan have been made, the debtor is entitled to a discharge of all claims provided for in the plan. The discharge does not apply to debts incurred after the bankruptcy petition was filed if they are not included in the plan.

In a Chapter 13 case, the only non-dischargeable debts include:

1. Alimony, separate maintenance and child support debts.

2. Student loan debts.

3. A debt for restitution included in the debtor's conviction of a crime, and/or a criminal fine.

4. A debt arising from the debtor's driving while under the influence of alcohol or drugs.

Nevertheless, if the debtor obtained the discharge by fraudulent means, an interested party may make a motion the court to revoke the discharge provided the motion is made within one year of the discharge, and that the party making the motion was unaware of the fraud until after the discharge took place.

Hardship Discharge

If circumstances arise that make it impossible for the Chapter 13 debtor to repay his or her debts, the court may be able to grant the debtor a hardship discharge of the remaining debt. The debtor must make a motion to the court for a hardship discharge. The creditors are entitled to notice of the motion and a hearing. The court generally takes into account the following criteria when determining whether to grant a hardship discharge:

1. Modification of the existing plan is not practical.

2. The value, on the effective date of the plan, of the property actually distributed to unsecured creditors under the plan is more than the amount that the creditors would have been paid if the estate had been liquidated on the effective date of the plan.

3. The debtor is unable to make the plan payments due to circumstances for which the debtor should not be held accountable.

The hardship discharge also does not discharge the debts that are nondischargeable under the full compliance discharge set forth above.

Closing the Chapter 13 Case

Once the payments under the Chapter 13 plan have been made, and a discharge of all eligible debts is obtained, the Chapter 13 case is closed.

APPENDICES

APPENDIX 1:

DIRECTORY OF UNITED STATES BANKRUPTCY COURTS

STATE	ADDRESS	TELEPHONE NUMBER
Alabama	P.O. Box 1805, 122 U.S. Courthouse, Anniston, AL 36201	205-237-5631
	500 S. 22nd Street, Birmingham, AL 35233	205-731-1615
	P.O. Box 1289, 222 Federal Courthouse, Decatur, AL 35601	205-353-2817
	P.O. Box 22865, Mobile, AL 36652	205-694-2390
	P.O. Box 1248, Suite 127, Montgomery, AL 36192	205-832-7250
	P.O. Box 3226, 351 Federal Building, 1118 24th Avenue, Tuscaloosa, AL 35401	205-752-5966
Alaska	P.O. Box 47, Federal Building, 701 "C" Street, Anchorage, AK 99513	907-261-6965
Arizona	U.S. Courthouse, 230 North First Avenue, Phoenix, AZ 85205	602-261-6965
	Acapulco Building, 120 W. Broadway, 2nd Floor, Tucson, AZ 85701	602-629-6304
Arkansas	P.O. Drawer 2381, 600 W. Capitol, Little Rock, AR 72203	501-378-6357
California	205 Post Office Building, Eureka, CA 95501	707-443-3131
	4310 Federal Building, 1130 O Street., Fresno, CA 93721	209-487-5217
	U.S. Courthouse, 312 N. Spring St., Room 906, Los Angeles, CA 94612	213-894-4696
	P.O. Box 5276, Modesto, CA 95352	209-521-5160
	214 Post Office Building, 13th & Alice Streets, Oakland, CA 84612	415-273-7212
	8038 U.S. Courthouse, 650 Capitol Mall, Sacramento, CA 95814	916-551-2662

STATE	ADDRESS	TELEPHONE NUMBER
	699 N. Arrowhead, Room 200, San Bernadino, CA 92401	714-383-5872
	U.S. Courthouse, 940 Front Street, Room 5-N-26, San Diego, CA 92189	619-293-6582
	P.O. Box 36053, 450 Golden Gate Avenue, San Francisco, CA 94102	415-556-2250
	280 South First Street, Room 3035, San Jose, CA 95113	408-291-7286
	506 Federal Building, 34 Civic Center Plaza, Santa Ana, CA 92701	714-836-2993
Colorado	1845 Sherman Street, 400 Columbine Building, Denver, CO 80203	303-844-4045
Connecticut	915 Lafayette Boulevard, Bridgeport, CT 06604	203-579-5808
	U.S. Courthouse, 450 Main Street, Hartford, CT 06103	203-722-2733
Delaware	Federal Building, 844 King Street, Lockbox 38, Wilmington, DE 19801	302-573-6174
District of Columbia	U.S. Courthouse, 3rd & Connecticut Avenues, Room 1130, Washington, DC 20001	202-535-7385
Florida	299 E. Broward Boulevard, Room 206A, Ft. Lauderdale, FL 33301	305-527-7224
	24 U.S. Post Office & Courthouse, P.O. Box 559, 311 West Monroe Street, Jacksonville, FL 32201	904-232-2852
	Federal Building, 51 SW First Avenue, Miami, FL 33130	305-536-5216
	598 Federal Courthouse Building, 80 N. Hughey Avenue, Orlando, FL 32801	305-648-6365
	700 Twiggs Street, Room 708, Tampa, FL 33602	813-228-2115
	701 Clanatis Street, West Palm Beach, FL 33401	305-655-6774
Georgia	R.B. Russell Building, 75 Spring Street SW, Room 1340, Atlanta, GA 30303	404-331-6490

STATE	ADDRESS	TELEPHONE NUMBER
	P.O. Box 2147, 904 Corporate Center, 233 12th Street, Columbus, GA 31902	404-527-1556
	P.O. Box 90, 126 U.S. Courthouse, Macon, GA 31202	912-746-2406
	P.O. Box 2328, Newnan, GA 30264	404-251-5583
	P.O. Box 5231, Rome, GA 30161	404-291-5639
	P.O. Box 8347, 213 U.s. Courthouse, Savannah, GA 31412	912-944-4105
Hawaii	P.O. Box 50121, New Federal Building, Honolulu, HI 96850	808-546-2180
Idaho	P.O. Box 2600, 304 N. 18th Street, Boise, ID 83701	208-334-1074
Illinois	U.S. Courthouse, 219 s. Dearborn Street, Chicago, IL 60604	312-435-5587
	P.O. Box 585, 302 Federal Building, 201 N. Vermilion Street, Danville, IL 61832	217-442-0660
	P.O. Box 309, 750 Missouri Avenue, 1st Floor, East St. Louis, IL 62202	618-482-9365
	Federal Building, 100 NE Monroe Street, Peoria, IL 61612	309-671-7035
	211 S. Court Street, Rockford, IL 61101	815-987-4202
	P.O. Box 2438, 327 U.s. courthouse, 600 E. Monroe Street, Springfield, IL 62705	217-492-4550
Indiana	352 Federal Building, Evansville, In 47708	812-465-6440
	221 Federal Building, 610 Connecticut Street, Gary, IN 46402	219-981-3335
	123 U.S. Courthouse, 46 E. Ohio Street, Indianapolis, IN 46204	317-269-6710
	222 U.S. Courthouse, 204 S. Main Street, South Bend, IN 46601	219-236-8247
Iowa	P.O. Box 4371, Federal Building & U.S. Courthouse, 1st Floor, Cedar Rapids, IA 52407	319-399-2473

STATE	ADDRESS	TELEPHONE NUMBER
	3118 U.S. Courthouse, Des Moines, IA 50309	515-284-6230
Kansas	155 Federal Building, L812 N. 7th Street, Kansas City, KS 66101	816-374-4741
	825 S.E. Quincy Street, Topeka, KS 66683	913-295-2750
	401 N. Market Street, Wichita, KS 67202	316-269-6486
Kentucky	P.O. Box 1050, Lexington, KY 40588	606-233-2608
	414 U.S. Courthouse, 601 W. Broadway, Louisville, KY 40202	502-582-5145
Louisiana	352 Florida Street, Room 301, Baton Rouge, LA 70801	504-389-0211
	500 Camp Street, Room C-104, New Orleans, LA 70130	504-389-6506
	252 Federal Building, Union & Vine Streets, Opelousas, LA 70570	318-948-3451
	4A 18 Federal Building, 500 Fannin Street, Shreveport, LA 71101	318-226-5267
Maine	P.O. Box 1109, 331 U.S. Courthouse, 202 Harlow Street, Bangor, ME 04401	207-945-0348
	U.S. Courthouse, 156 Federal Street, Portland, ME 04112	207-780-3482
Maryland	U.S. Courthouse, 101 W. Lombard Street, Baltimore, MD 21201	301-962-2688
	451 Huntingford Drive, Rockville, MD 20850	301-443-7010
Massachusetts	212 John W. McCormick, Post Office & Courthouse, Boston, MA 02109	617-223-2937
	512 Federal Building, 595 Main Street, Worcester, MA 01601	617-793-0518
Michigan	P.O. Box X911, 100 Washington, Bay City, MI 48707	517-892-1506
	1060 U.S. Courthouse, 231 W. Lafayette, Detroit, MI 48226	313-226-7064

STATE	ADDRESS	TELEPHONE NUMBER
	102A Federal Building, 600 Church Street, Flint, MI 48502	313-234-5621
	P.O. Box 3310, 792 Federal Building, 110 Michigan Street N.W., Grand Rapids, MI 49501	616-456-2693
	221 W. Washington Street, Marquette, MI 49855	906-226-2117
Minnesota	416 U.S. Post Office & Courthouse, Duluth, MN 55802	218-727-6692
	204 U.S. Post Office, 118 S. Mills Street, Fergus Falls, MN 56537	218-739-4671
	600 Galaxy Building, 330 Second Avenue South, Minneapolis, MN 55401	612-349-5155
	629 Federal Building, 316 N. Robert Street, St. Paul, MN 55101	612-725-7184
Mississippi	P.O. Drawer 867, Arberdeen, MS 39730	601-965-5301
	P.O. Box 1280, 231 Main Street, Biloxi, MS 39533	601-432-5542
	P.O. Drawer 2448, Jackson, MS 39205	601-965-5301
Missouri	U.S. Courthouse, 811 Grand Avenue, Kansas City, MO 64106	816-374-3321
	730 U.S. Courthouse, 1114 Market Street, St. Louis, MO 63101	314-425-4222
Montana	Federal Building, 400 N. Main Street, Room 111, Butte, MT 59701	406-782-3354
	Great Falls Post Office Building, 215 First Avenue North, Room 25, Great Falls, MT 59401	406-781-3811
Nebraska	P.O. Box 428 Downtown Station, New Federal Building, 215 N. 17th Street, Omaha, NB 68101	402-221-4687
Nevada	U.S. Courthouse, 300 Las Vegas Boulevard South, Room 300, Las Vegas, NV 89101	702-388-6257
	4050 Federal Building & Courthouse, 300 Booth Street, Reno, NV 89509	702-784-5559
New Hampshire	275 Chestnut Street, Manchester, NH 03101	603-666-7532

STATE	ADDRESS	TELEPHONE NUMBER
New Jersey	401 Market Street, Camden, NJ 08101	609-757-5023
	970 Broad Street, Newark, NJ 07102	201-645-2630
	U.S. Post Office & Courthouse, 402 E. State Street, Trenton, NJ 08608	609-989-2126
New Mexico	P.O. Box 546, 500 Gold Avenue, 9th floor, Albuquerque, NM 87103	505-766-2051
New York	P.O. Box 398, Albany, NY 12201	518-472-4226
	75 Clinton Street, Brooklyn, NY 11201	718-330-2188
	U.S. Courthouse, 68 Court Street, Room 310, Buffalo, NY 14202	716-846-4130
	601 Veterans Highway, Hauppauge, NY 11787	516-361-8601
	40 Foley Square, Room 230, New York, NY 10007	212-791-0143
	P.O. Box 1000, 176 Church Street, Poughkeepsie, NY 12602	914-452-4200
	234 Federal Building, Rochester, NY 14614	716-263-3148
	311 U.S. Courthouse, Utica, NY 13501	315-793-8176
	1635 Privado Road, Westbury, NY 11590	516-832-8801
	U.S. Courthouse, 300 Quarropas Street, White Plains, NY 10601	914-390-4060
North Carolina	401 W. Trade Street, Charlotte, NC 28202	704-371-6103
	P.O. Box 26100, Greensboro, NC 27420	919-333-5647
	P.O. Drawer 2807, Wilson, NC 27834	919-237-0248
North Dakota	P.O. Box 1110, Fargo, ND 58107	701-237-5771
Ohio	2 S. Main Street, Akron, OH 44308	216-375-5766
	107 F.T. Bow Building, 201 Cleveland Avenue SW, Canton, OH 44702	216-489-4426
	735 U.S. Courthouse, 100 E. 5th Street, Cincinnati, OH 45202	513-684-2572

STATE	ADDRESS	TELEPHONE NUMBER
	U.S. Courthouse, Public Square & Superior Avenues, Room 427, Cleveland, OH 44114	216-522-7555
	124 U.S. Courthouse, 85 Marconi Boulevard, Columbus, OH 43215	614-469-2087
	705 Federal Building & U.S. Courthouse, 200 W. 2nd Street, Dayton, OH 45402	513-225-2516
	113 U.S. Courthouse, 1716 Spielbusch Avenue, Toledo, OH 43624	419-259-6440
	P.O. Box 147, U.S. Post Office Building, Youngstown, OH 44501	2160746-7702
Oklahoma	Old Post Office Building, 201 Dean A. McGee Avenue, 7th Floor, Oklahoma City, OK 73102	405-231-5143
	P.O. Box 1347, U.S. Post Office & Federal Building, Okmulgee, OK 74447	918-758-0126
	4-540 U.S. Courthouse, 333 W. 4th Street, Tulsa, OK 74103	918-581-7181
Oregon	P.O. Box 1335, 404 Federal Building, 211 E. 7th Street, Eugene, OR 97401	503-687-6448
	900 Orbanco Building, 1001 S.W. 5th Avenue, Portland, OR 97204	503-221-2231
Pennsylvania	P.O. Box 1755, 314 U.S. Courthouse, Erie, PA 16507	814-453-7580
	P.O. Box 908, Federal Building, 3rd & Walnut Streets, Harrisburg, PA 17108	717-782-2260
	3726 U.S. Courthouse, 601 Market Street, Philadelphia, PA 19106	215-597-1644
	4108 E. Shore Office Building, 45 S. Front Street, Reading, PA 19602	215-375-0930
	217 Federal Building, 197 S. Main Street, Wilkes-Barre, PA 18701	717-826-6450
Rhode Island	Federal Center, 380 Westminster Mall, Providence, RI 02903	401-528-4477
South Carolina	P.O. Box 1448, Columbia, SC 29202	803-765-5211

STATE	ADDRESS	TELEPHONE NUMBER
South Dakota	Federal Building & Courthouse, 400 S. Phillips Avenue, Sioux Falls, SD 57102	605-336-9903
Tennessee	P.O. Box 1189, Martin Luther King Boulevard & Georgia Avenue, Chattanooga, TN 37401	615-226-2126
	Plaza Tower, Suite 1501, Knoxville, TN 37929	615-673-4525
	P.O. Box 1527, Jackson, TN 38302	901-424-9751
	969 Madison Avenue, Suite 1200, TN 38104	901-521-3204
	207 Customs House, 701 Broadway, Nashville, TN 37203	615-736-5590
Texas	200 W. 8th Street, Austin, TX 78701	512-482-5237
	521 Starr, Room 101, Corpus Christi, TX 78401	512-888-3142
	14-A-7 U.S. Courthouse, 1100 Commerce Street, Dallas, TX 75242	214-767-0814
	P.O. Box 1349, Del Rio, TX 78840	512-775-2021
	511 E. San Antonio, El Paso, TX 799-1	915-541-7810
	504 U.S. Courthouse, Fort Worth, TX 76102	817-334-3269
	U.S. Courthouse, 515 Rusk Avenue, Houston, TX 77002	713-221-9590
	C-110 Federal Building, 1205 Texas Avenue, Lubbock, TX 79401	806-743-7336
	P.O. Box 10708, Midland, TX 79702	915-683-2001
	P.O. Box 191, Pecos, TX 79772	915-445-4228
	P.O. Box 1439, Post Office Building, 1615 E. Houston Street, Alamo Plaza, San Antonio, TX 78295	512-229-6720
	211 W. Ferguson Street, Tyler, TX 75702	215-592-1212
	P.O. Box 608, Waco, TX 76703	817-756-0307
Utah	350 S. Main Street, Salt Lake City, UT 84101	801-524-5157
Vermont	P.O. Box 865, Opera House, Rutland, VT 05701	802-773-0219

STATE	ADDRESS	TELEPHONE NUMBER
Virginia	City Bank & Trust Building, 206 N. Washington Street, Suite 408, Alexandria, VA 22314	703-557-1716
	P.O. Box 1326, Federal Building, Hansonburg, VA 22801	703-434-8327
	205 Federal Building, Lynchburg, VA 24505	804-845-0317
	P.O. Box 497, Newport News, VA 23607	804-247-0196
	414 U.S. Courthouse, Norfolk, VA 23510	804-441-6651
	P.O. Box 676, 1100 E. Main Street, Room 324, Richmond, VA 23206	804-771-2878
	P.O. Box 2390, New Federal Building, 2nd Street & Franklin Road S.W., Roanoke, VA 24010	703-982-6391
Washington	220 U.S. Courthouse, 1010 5th Avenue, Seattle, WA 98104	206-442-2751
	P.O. Box 2164, U.S. Courthouse, 904 W. Riverside Avenue, Room 321, Spokane, WA 92201	509-456-3830
	P.O. Box 1797, 224 Post Office Building, Tacoma, WA 98402	206-593-6310
West Virginia	P.O. Box 3924, Charleston, WV 25339	304-347-5114
	P.O. Box 70, 12th & Chapline Streets, Wheeling, WV 26003	304-233-1655
Wisconsin	510 S. Barstow Street, Eau Claire, WI 54701	715-834-3941
	P.O. Box 548, 120 N. Henry, Madison, WI 53701	608-264-5178
	216 Federal Building, 517 E. Wisconsin Avenue, Milwaukee, WI 53202	414-291-3293
Wyoming	111 S. Wolcott Street, Casper, WY 82601	307-261-5440
	P.O. Box 1107, New Post Office & Courthouse, 2120 Capitol Avenue, Cheyenne, WY 82003	307-722-2191

APPENDIX 2:

SAMPLE VOLUNTARY BANKRUPTCY PETITION

Form B1, P1 (12-94)

FORM 1 VOLUNTARY PETITION

United States Bankruptcy Court District of	VOLUNTARY PETITION
IN RE (Name of debtor-If individual, enter Last, First, Middle)	NAME OF JOINT DEBTOR (Spouse) (Last, First, Middle)
ALL OTHER NAMES used by the debtor in the last 6 years (including married, maiden and trade names)	ALL OTHER NAMES used by the joint debtor in the last 6 years (include married, maiden and trade names)
SOC. SEC./TAX I.D. NO. (If more than one, state all)	SOC. SEC./TAX I.D. NO. (If more than one, state all)
STREET ADDRESS OF DEBTOR (No. and street, city, state, zip)	STREET ADDRESS OF JOINT DEBTOR (No. and street, city, state, zip)
COUNTY OF RESIDENCE OR PRINCIPAL PLACE OF BUSINESS	COUNTY OF RESIDENCE OR PRINCIPAL PLACE OF BUSINESS
MAILING ADDRESS OF DEBTOR (If different from street address)	_ OF JOINT DEBTOR (If different from street address)

SAMPLE

LOCATION OF PRINCIPLE ASSETS OF BUSINESS DEBTOR (If different from addresses listed above)	VENUE (Check one box)

☐ Debtor has been domiciled or has had a residence, principal place of business or principal assets in this District for 180 days immediately preceding the date of this petition or for a longer part of such 180 days than in any other District.
☐ There is a bankruptcy case concerning debtor's affiliate, general partner or partnership pending in this district

INFORMATION REGARDING DEBTOR (Check Applicable boxes)

TYPE OF DEBTOR (Check one box)	CHAPTER OR SECTION OF BANKRUPTCY CODE UNDER WHICH THE PETITION IS FILED (Check one box)

TYPE OF DEBTOR (Check one box)
☐ Individual ☐ Corporation Publicly Held
☐ Joint (H&W) ☐ Corporation Not Publicly Held
☐ Partnership ☐ Municipality
☐ Other _____

CHAPTER OR SECTION OF BANKRUPTCY CODE UNDER WHICH THE PETITION IS FILED (Check one box)
☐ Chapter 7 ☐ Chapter 11 ☐ Chapter 13
☐ Chapter 9 ☐ Chapter 12 ☐ § 304-Case Ancillary to Foreign Proceeding
SMALL BUSINESS (Ch.11 only)
☐ Debtor is a small business as defined in 11 U.S.C. § 101.

NATURE OF DEBT (Check one box)
☐ Non-Business Consumer ☐ Business - Complete A&B below

☐ Debtor is and elects to be considered a small business under 11 U.S.C. § 1121(e). (optional)

A. TYPE OF BUSINESS (Check one box)
☐ Farming ☐ Transportation ☐ Commodity Broker
☐ Professional ☐ Manufacturing/Mining ☐ Construction
☐ Retail/Wholesale ☐ Stockbroker ☐ Real Estate
☐ Railroad ☐ Other Business

FILING FEE (Check one box)
☐ Filing fee attached.
☐ Filing fee to be paid in installments. (Applicable to individuals only) Must attach signed application for the court's consideration certifying that the debtor is unable to pay fee except in installments. Rule 1006(b); see Official Form Number 3

B. BRIEFLY DESCRIBE NATURE OF BUSINESS

NAME AND ADDRESS OF LAW FIRM OR ATTORNEY

Telephone No.

STATISTICAL ADMINISTRATIVE INFORMATION (28 U.S.C. § 604) (Estimates only) (Check applicable boxes)	NAME(S) OF ATTORNEY(S) DESIGNATED TO REPRESENT THE DEBTOR (Print or Type)

☐ Debtor estimates that funds will be available for distribution to unsecured creditors.
☐ Debtor estimates that after any exempt property is excluded and administrative expenses paid, there will be no funds available for distribution to unsecured creditors.

☐ Debtor is not represented by an attorney. Telephone no. of debtor not represented by an attorney: ( )

ESTIMATED NUMBER OF CREDITORS						THIS SPACE FOR COURT USE ONLY
☐ 1-15	☐ 16-49	☐ 50-99	☐ 100-199	☐ 200-999	☐ 1000-over	

ESTIMATED ASSETS (in thousands of dollars)
☐ Under 50 ☐ 50-99 ☐ 100-499 ☐ 500-999 ☐ 1000-9999 ☐ 10,000-99,000 ☐ 100,000-over

ESTIMATED LIABILITIES (in thousands of dollars)
☐ Under 50 ☐ 50-99 ☐ 100-499 ☐ 500-999 ☐ 1000-9999 ☐ 10,000-99,000 ☐ 100,000-over

ESTIMATED NUMBER OF EMPLOYEES - CH 11 & 12 ONLY
☐ 0 ☐ 1-19 ☐ 20-99 ☐ 100-999 ☐ 1000-over

ESTIMATED NO. OF EQUITY SECURITY HOLDERS - CH 11 & 12 ONLY
☐ 0 ☐ 1-19 ☐ 20-99 ☐ 100-999 ☐ 1000-over

Form B1, P2 (12-94)

Julius Blumberg, Inc. NYC 10013

Name of Debtor: _____   Case No. _____
(Court use only)

FILING OF PLAN   For Chapter 7,11, 12 and 13 cases only. Check appropriate box.

☐ A Copy of debtor's proposed plan dated _____ is attached.   ☐ Debtor intends to file a plan within the time allowed by statute, rule, or order of the court.

PRIOR BANKRUPTCY CASE FILED WITHIN LAST 6 YEARS (If more than one, attach additional sheet)

Location Where Filed	Case Number	Date Filed

PENDING BANKRUPTCY CASE FILED BY ANY SPOUSE, PARTNER, OR AFFILIATE OF THIS DEBTOR (If more than one, attach additional sheet.)

Name of Debtor	Case Number	Date
Relationship	District	Judge

REQUEST FOR RELIEF   Debtor is eligible for and requests relief in accordance with the chapter of title 11, United States Code, specified in this petition.

SIGNATURES

ATTORNEY   Signature   X _____   Date _____

INDIVIDUAL/JOINT DEBTOR(S)

I declare under penalty of perjury that the information provided in this petition is true and correct

X _____
Signature of Debtor

_____
Date

X _____
Signature of Joint Debtor

_____
Date

OR PARTNERSHIP DEBTOR

I declare that the information provided in this petition is true and been authorized to file this petition on

_____
orized Individual

_____
or Type Name of Authorized Individual

_____
Title of Individual Authorized by Debtor to File this Petition

_____
Date

If debtor is a corporation filing under chapter 11, Exhibit "A" is attached and made part of this petition.

SAMPLE

TO BE COMPLETED BY INDIVIDUAL CHAPTER 7 DEBTOR WITH PRIMARILY CONSUMER DEBTS (See P.L. 98-353 § 322)

I am aware that I may proceed under chapter 7, 11, or 12, or 13 of title 11, United States Code, understand the relief available under each such chapter, and choose to proceed under chapter 7 of such title.

If I am represented by an attorney, exhibit "B" has been completed.

X _____   _____
Signature of Debtor   Date

X _____   _____
Signature of Joint Debtor   Date

EXHIBIT "B"

(To be completed by attorney for individual chapter 7 debtor(s) with primarily consumer debts.)

I, the attorney for the debtor(s) named in the foregoing petition, declare that I have informed the debtor(s) that (he, she, or they) may proceed under chapter 7, 11, 12, or 13 of title 11, United States Code, and have explained the relief available under such chapter.

X _____   _____
Signature of Attorney   Date

CERTIFICATION AND SIGNATURE OF NON-ATTORNEY BANKRUPTCY PETITION PREPARER (See 11 U.S.C. § 110)

I certify that I am a bankruptcy petition preparer as defined in 11 U.S.C. § 110, that I have prepared this document for compensation, and that I have provided the debtor with a copy of this document.

_____
Printed or Typed Name of Bankruptcy Petition Preparer

_____
Social Security Number

_____
Address   Tel.No.

Names and Social Security numbers of all other individuals who prepared or assisted in preparing this document:

If more than one person prepared this document, attach additional signed sheets conforming to the appropriate Official Form for each person.

X _____
Signature of Bankruptcy Petition Preparer

A bankruptcy petition preparer's failure to comply with the provisions of title 11 and the Federal Rules of Bankruptcy Procedure may result in fines or imprisonment or both. 11 U.S.C. § 110; 18 U.S.C. § 156.

3066-2 © 1991 JULIUS BLUMBERG, INC., NYC 10013

APPENDIX 3:

SAMPLE CREDITOR'S PROOF OF CLAIM

B10 (Official Form 10)
(Rev. 12/94)

United States Bankruptcy Court _____ District of _____	PROOF OF CLAIM
In re (Name of Debtor)	Case Number

NOTE: This form should not be used to make a claim for an administrative expense arising after the commencement of the case. A "request" for payment of an administrative expense may be filed pursuant to 11 U.S.C. § 503.

Name of Creditor (The person or other entity to whom the debtor owes money or property)	☐ Check box if you are aware that any-one else has filed a proof of claim relating to your claim. Attach copy of statement giving particulars.	
Name and Address Where Notices Should be Sent	☐ Check box if you have never received any notices from the bankruptcy court in this case.	
	☐ Check box if the address differs from the address on the envelope sent to you by the court.	THIS SPACE IS FOR COURT USE ONLY
Telephone No.		

ACCOUNT OR OTHER NUMBER BY WHICH CREDITOR IDENTIFIES DEBTOR:	Check here if this claim ☐ replaces ☐ amends a previously filed claim, dated:_____

1. BASIS FOR CLAIM

☐ Goods sold	☐ Retiree benefits as defined in 11 U.S.C. § 1114(a)
☐ Services performed	☐ Wages, salaries, and compensation (Fill out below)
☐ Money loaned	Your social security number_____
☐ Personal injury/wrongful death	Unpaid compensation for services performed
☐ Taxes	from_____ to _____
☐ Other (Describe briefly)	(date) (date)

2. DATE DEBT WAS INCURRED	3. IF COURT, JUDGMENT, DATE OBTAINED:

4. CLASSIFICATION OF CLAIM. Under the Bankruptcy Code all claims are classified as one or more of the following: (1) Unsecured nonpriority, (2) Unsecured Priority, (3) Secured. It is possible for part of a claim to be in one category and part in another.
CHECK THE APPROPRIATE BOX OR BOXES that best describe your claim and STATE THE AMOUNT OF THE CLAIM AT TIME CASE FILED.

☐ SECURED CLAIM $ _____ Attach evidence of perfection of security interest Brief Description of Collateral: ☐ Real Estate ☐ Motor Vehicle ☐ Other (Describe briefly) Amount of arrearage and other charges at time case filed included in secured claim above, if any $ _____	☐ Wages, salaries, or commissions (up to $4000),* earned not more than 90 days before filing of the bankruptcy petition or cessation of the debtor's business, whichever is earlier—11 U.S.C. § 507(a)(3)
	☐ Contributions to an employee benefit plan—11 U.S.C. § 507(a)(4)
	☐ Up to $1,800* of deposits toward purchase, lease, or rental of property or services for personal, family, or household use—11 U.S.C. § 507(a)(6)
☐ UNSECURED NONPRIORITY CLAIM $ _____ A claim is unsecured if there is no collateral or lien on property of the debtor securing the claim or to the extent that the value of such property is less than the amount of the claim.	☐ Alimony, maintenance, or support owed to a spouse, former spouse, or child—11 U.S.C. § 507(a)(7)
	☐ Taxes or penalties of governmental units—11 U.S.C. § 507(a)(8)
☐ UNSECURED PRIORITY CLAIM $ _____ Specify the priority of the claim.	☐ Other—Specify applicable paragraph of 11 U.S.C. § 507(a)_____ *Amounts are subject to adjustment on 4/1/98 and every 3 years thereafter with respect to cases commenced on or after the date of adjustment.

5. TOTAL AMOUNT OF CLAIM AT TIME CASE FILED: $ _____ (Unsecured) $ _____ (Secured) $ _____ (Priority) $ _____ (Total)

☐ Check this box if claim includes charges in addition to the principal amount of the claim. Attach itemized statement of all additional charges.

6. CREDITS AND SETOFFS: The amount of all payments on this claim has been credited and deducted for the purpose of making this proof of claim. In filing this claim, claimant has deducted all amounts that claimant owes to debtor.	THIS SPACE IS FOR COURT USE ONLY
7. SUPPORTING DOCUMENTS: *Attach copies of supporting documents,* such as promissory notes, purchase orders, invoices, itemized statements of running accounts, contracts, court judgments, or evidence of security interests. If the documents are not available, explain. If the documents are voluminous, attach a summary.	
8. TIME-STAMPED COPY: To receive an acknowledgement of the filing of your claim, enclose a stamped, self-addressed envelope and copy of this proof of claim.	
Date	Sign and print the name and title, if any, of the creditor or other person authorized to file this claim (attach copy of power of attorney, if any)

Penalty for presenting fraudulent claim: Fine of up to $500,000 or imprisonment for up to 5 years, or both. 18 U.S.C. §§ 152 and 3571.

APPENDIX 4:

SAMPLE APPLICATION AND ORDER TO PAY FILING FEE IN INSTALLMENTS

APPLICATION AND ORDER TO PAY FILING FEE IN INSTALLMENTS

Pursuant to Fed R Bankr P 1006, application is made for permission to pay the filing fee on the following terms:

$_____ with the filing of the petition, and the balance of

$_____ in _____ installments, as follows:

$_____ on or before _____

$_____ on or before _____

$_____ on or before _____

$_____ on or before _____

I certify I am unable to pay the filing fee except in installments. I further certify I have not paid any money or transferred any property to an attorney or any other person for services in connection with this case or in connection with any other pending bankruptcy case, and I will not make any payment or transfer any property for services in connection with the case until the filing fee is paid in full.

Date: _____   _____
                                          Applicant

                               _____
                                   Attorney for Applicant

CERTIFICATION AND SIGNATURE OF NON-ATTORNEY BANKRUPTCY PETITION PREPARER

I certify that I am a bankruptcy petition preparer as defined in 11 USC § 110, that I have prepared this debtor's petition for compensation, and I have provided the debtor with a copy of this document.

_____   _____
Printed or Typed Name of Petition Preparer   Social Security No.

Address:_____   _____
_____   Name and Social Security No. of Person
_____   Assisting in Preparing Petition (If more
                                           than one person prepared this petition,
                                           attach a copy of Official Form for each).

_____   _____
Signature of Bankruptcy Petition Preparer   Date
A preparer's failure to comply with title 11 and the Fed R Bankr P may result in fines, imprisonment or both. 11 USC § 110, 18 USC § 156.

ORDER

ORDERED, that the Debtor pay the filing fee in installments on the terms set forth in the above application.

ORDERED, that until the filing fee is paid in full, the Debtor shall not pay or transfer, and no person shall accept, any money or transfer of property for services, in connection with this case.

Dated:_____
        White Plains, New York   _____
                                          United States Bankruptcy Judge

APPENDIX 5:

SAMPLE SUMMONS TO DEBTOR IN INVOLUNTARY BANKRUPTCY CASE

B2501
(6-91)

United States Bankruptcy Court

_____ District of _____ _____

In re

Bankruptcy Case No.

Debtor*
Social Security No.   :
Employer Tax I.D. No.:

SUMMONS TO DEBTOR IN INVOLUNTARY CASE

To the above named debtor:

A petition under title 11, United States Code was filed against you on _____
(date)
in this bankruptcy court, requesting an order for relief under chapter _____ of the Bankruptcy Code (title

11 of the United States Code).

YOU ARE SUMMONED and required to submit to the clerk of the bankruptcy court a motion or

answer to the petition within 20 days after the service of this summons. A copy of the petition is attached.

Address of Clerk

At the same time you must also serve a copy of your motion or answer on petitioner's attorney.

Name and Address of Petitioner's Attorney

If you make a motion, your time to serve an answer is governed by Bankruptcy Rule 1011(c).

If you fail to respond to this summons, the order for relief will be entered.

_____
Clerk of the Bankruptcy Court

By: _____

_____   _____
Date   Deputy Clerk

*Set forth all names, including trade names, used by the debtor within the last 6 years. (Bankruptcy Rule 1005). For joint debtors, set forth both
social security numbers.

Case No._____

CERTIFICATION OF SERVICE

I,   ,
of**   ,
certify:

That I am, and at all times hereinafter mentioned was, more than 18 years of age;
That on the   day of   , 19   ,
I served a copy of the within summons, together with the petition filed in this case, on

the debtor in this case, by [*describe here the mode of service*]

the said debtor at

I certify under penalty of perjury that the foregoing is true and correct.

Executed on _____   _____
                           [Date]   *[Signature]*

_____
**State mailing address*

APPENDIX 6:

SAMPLE ORDER RESTRAINING CREDITORS

UNITED STATES BANKRUPTCY COURT
Southern District of New York

In re

Case No.

Debtor(s)
Social Security No.:
Employer Tax ID No.:

ORDER RESTRAINING CREDITORS

It appearing that the above debtor filed an original petition under Chapter _____ of

the Bankruptcy Code on _____, and it further appearing that under

the Bankruptcy Code, creditors are stayed from taking any action against the debtor,

IT IS HEREBY

ORDERED, that the creditors of the above debtor be and they hereby are restrained

from taking any action which is in violation of the provisions of the Bankruptcy Code.

Dated: NEW YORK, NEW YORK

_____
Bankruptcy Judge

APPENDIX 7:

AUTOMATIC STAY PROVISIONS UNDER SECTION 362 OF THE BANKRUPTCY CODE

SECTION 362. Automatic stay

(a) Except as provided in subsection (b) of this section, a petition filed under section 301, 302, or 303 of this title, or an application filed under section 5(a)(3) of the Securities Investor Protection Act of 1970 (15 U.S.C. 78eee(a)(3)), operates as a stay, applicable to all entities, of:

(1) the commencement or continuation, including the issuance or employment of process, of a judicial, administrative, or other action or proceeding against the debtor that was or could have been commenced before the commencement of the case under this title, or to recover a claim against the debtor that arose before the commencement of the case under this title;

(2) the enforcement, against the debtor or against property of the estate, or a judgment obtained before the commencement of the case under this title;

(3) any act to obtain possession of property of the estate or of property from the estate or to exercise control over property of the estate;

(4) any act to create, perfect, or enforce any lien against property of the estate;

(5) any act to create, perfect, or enforce against property of the debtor any lien to the extent that such lien secures a claim that arose before the commencement of the case under this title;

(6) any act to collect, assess, or recover a claim against the debtor that arose before the commencement of the case under this title;

(7) the setoff of any debt owing to the debtor that arose before the commencement of the case under this title against: any claim against the debtor; and

(8) the commencement or continuation of a proceeding before the United States Tax Court concerning the debtor.

(b) The filing of a petition under section 301, 302, or 303 of this title, or of an application under section 5(a)(3) of the Securities Investor Protection Act of 1970 (15 U.S.C. 78eee(a)(3)), does not operate as a stay:

(1) under subsection (a) of this section, of the commencement or continuation of a criminal action or proceeding against the debtor;

(2) under subsection (a) of this section, of the collection of alimony, maintenance, or support from property that is not property of the estate;

(3) under subsection (a) of this section, of any act to perfect an interest in property to the extent that the trustee's rights and powers are subject to such perfection under section 546(b) of this title or to the extent that such act is accomplished within the period provided under section 547(e)(2)(A) of this title;

(4) under subsection (a)(1) of this section, of the commencement or continuation of an action or proceeding by a governmental unit to enforce such governmental unit's police or regulatory power;

(5) under subsection (a)(2) of this section, of the enforcement of a judgment, other than a money judgment, obtained in an action or proceeding by a governmental unit to enforce such governmental unit's police or regulatory power;

(6) under subsection (a) of this section, of the setoff by a commodity broker, forward contract merchant, stockbroker, financial institutions, or securities clearing agency of any mutual debt and claim under or in connection with commodity contracts, as defined in section 761(4) of this title, forward contracts, or securities contracts, as defined in section 741(7) of this title, that constitutes the setoff of a claim against the debtor for a margin payment, as defined in section 741(5) or 761(15) of this title, or settlement payment, as defined in section 741(8) of this title, arising out of commodity contracts, forward contracts, or securities contracts against cash, securities or other property held by or due from such commodity broker, forward contract merchant, stockbroker, financial institutions, or securities clearing agency to margin, guarantee, secure, or settle commodity contracts, forward contracts, or securities contracts;

(7) under subsection (a) of this section, of the setoff by a repo participant, of any mutual debt and claim under or in connection with repurchase agreements that constitutes the setoff of a claim against the debtor for a margin payment, as defined in section 741(5) or 761(15) of this title, or settlement payment, as defined in section 741(8) of this title, arising out of repurchase agreements against cash, securities, or other property held by or due from such repo participant to margin, guarantee, secure or settle repurchase agreements;

(8) under subsection (a) of this section, of the commencement of any action by the Secretary of Housing and Urban Development to foreclose a mortgage or deed of trust in any case in which the mortgage or deed of trust held by the Secretary is insured or was formerly insured under the National Housing Act and covers property, or combinations of property, consisting of five or more living units;

(9) under subsection (a) of this section, of the issuance to the debtor by a governmental unit of a notice of tax deficiency;

(10) under subsection (a) of this section, of any act by a lessor to the debtor under a lease of nonresidential real property that has terminated by the expiration of the stated term of the lease before the commencement of or during a case under this title to obtain possession of such property; or

(11) under subsection (a) of this section, of the presentment of a negotiable instrument and the giving of notice of and protesting dishonor of such an instrument;

(12) under subsection (a) of this section, after the date which is 90 days after the filing of such petition, of the commencement or continuation, and conclusion to the entry of final judgment, of an action which involves a debtor subject to reorganization pursuant to chapter 11 of this title and which was brought by the Secretary of Transportation under the Ship Mortgage Act, 1920 (46 App. U.S.C. 911 et seq.) (including distribution of any proceeds of sale) to foreclose a preferred ship or fleet mortgage, or a security interest in or relating to a vessel or vessel under construction, held by the Secretary of Transportation under section 207 or title Xi of the Merchant Marine Act,1936 (46 App. U.S.C. 1117 and 1271 et seq., respectively), or under applicable State law; or

(13) under subsection (a) of this section, after the date which is 90 days after the filing of such petition, of the commencement or continuation, and conclusion to the entry of final judgment, of an action which involves a debtor subject to reorganization pursuant to chapter 11 of this title and which was brought by the Secretary of Commerce under the Ship Mortgage Act, 1920 (46 App. U.S.C. 911 et seq.) (including distribution of any proceeds of sale) to foreclose a preferred ship or fleet mortgage in a vessel or a mortgage, deed of trust, or other security interest in a fishing facility held by the Secretary of Commerce under section 207 or title XI of the Merchant Marine Act, 1936 (46 App. U.S.C. 1117 and 1271 et seq., respectively). The provisions of paragraphs (12) and (13) of this subsection shall apply with respect to any such petition filed on or before December 31, 1989.

(c) Except as provided in subsections (d), (e), and (1) of this section:

(1) the stay of an act against property of the estate under subsection (a) of this section continues until such property is no longer property of the estate; and

(2) the stay of any other act under subsection (a) of this section continues until the earliest of:

(A) the time the case is closed;

(B) the time the case is dismissed; or

(C) if the case is a case under chapter 7 of this title concerning an individual or a case under chapter 9, 11, 12, or 13 of this title, the time a discharge is granted or denied.

(d) On request of a party in interest and after notice and a hearing, the court shall grant relief from the stay provided under subsection (a) of this section, such as by terminating, annulling, modifying, or conditioning such stay:

(1) for cause, including the lack of adequate protection of an interest in property of such party in interest; or

(2) with respect to a stay of an act against property under subsection (a) of this section, if:

(A) the debtor does not have an equity in such property; and

(B) such property is not necessary to an effective reorganization.

(e) Thirty days after a request under subsection (d) of this section for relief from the stay of any act against property of the estate under subsection (a) of this section, such stay is terminated with respect to the party in interest making such request, unless the court, after notice and a hearing, orders such stay continued in effect pending the conclusion of, or as a result of, a final hearing and determination under subsection (d) of this section. A hearing under this subsection may be a preliminary hearing, or may be consolidated with the final hearing under subsection (d) of this section. The court shall order such stay continued in effect pending the conclusion of the final hearing under subsection (d) of this section if there is a reasonable likelihood that the party opposing relief from such stay will prevail at the conclusion of such final hearing. If the hearing under this subsection is a preliminary hearing, then such final hearing shall be commenced not later than thirty days after the conclusion of such preliminary hearing.

(f) Upon request of a party in interest, the court with or without a hearing, shall grant such relief from the stay provided under subsection (a) of this section as is necessary to prevent irreparable damage to the interest of an entity in property, if such interest will suffer such damage before there is an opportunity for notice and a hearing under subsection (d) or (e) of this section.

(g) In any hearing under subsection (d) or (e) of this section concerning relief from the stay of any act under subsection (a) of this section:

(1) The party requesting such relief has the burden of proof on the issue of the debtor's equity in property; and

(2) The party opposing such relief has the burden of proof on all other issues.

(h) An individual injured by any willful violation of a stay provided by this section shall recover actual damages, including costs and attorneys' fees, and, in appropriate circumstances, may recover punitive damages.

APPENDIX 8:

FEDERAL EXEMPTIONS UNDER §522(d) OF THE BANKRUPTCY CODE

EXEMPTION	DESCRIPTION
Alimony	Alimony and child support needed for support.
Homestead	Real property or mobile home or cooperative used as a residence valued up to $15,000.
Insurance	Unmatured life insurance contract; life insurance policy with loan value up to $8,000; disability
Pensions	ERISA-qualified needed for support.
Personal Property	Motor vehicle valued up to $2,400; animals; crops; clothing; appliances; books; furnishings; household goods; music instruments valued up to $400 per item; jewelry valued up to $1,000; health aids; wrongful death recoveries valued up to $15,000 not including pain and suffering and pecuniary loss; lost earnings payments.
Public Benefits	Unemployment compensation; social security benefits; other public assistance.
Tools of the Trade	Implements, books and trade tools valued up to $1500.
Wild Card	Any property valued up to $800; $7500 in any property less any amount of homestead exemption.

APPENDIX 9:

NON-BANKRUPTCY FEDERAL EXEMPTIONS

EXEMPTION	STATUTE
Civil Service Retirement Benefits	5 U.S.C. §§729 and 2265
Foreign Service Retirement and Disability Benefits	22 U.S.C. §1104
Injury or Death Compensation Benefits Related to War-risk Hazards	442 U.S.C. §1717
Longshoremen's and Harbor Worker's Death and Disability Benefits	33 U.S.C. §916
Railroad Retirement Act Annuities and Pensions	45 U.S.C. §228
Social Security Benefits	42 U.S.C. §407
Veterans Benefits	45 U.S.C. §352
Wages from Employment as a Fisherman or Seaman	46 U.S.C. §601

APPENDIX 10:

TABLE OF STATE STATUTES GOVERNING BANKRUPTCY EXEMPTIONS

STATE	STATUTE	FEDERAL BANKRUPTCY CODE EXEMPTIONS ALLOWED
Alabama	Alabama Code §6-10-2 (homestead); §6-10-5 (burial place); §6-10-6 (personal property)	No
Alaska	Alaska Statutes §09.38.010 (homestead); §09.38.017 (retirement benefits); §§09.38.015 et seq. (personal property)	No
Arizona	Arizona Revised Statutes Annotated §33-101 (homestead); §§33-1121 et seq. (personal property)	No
Arkansas	Arkansas Statutes Annotated §§16-66-210 and 16-66-218b (homestead); §16-22-218a (property); §16-66-218b (personal property)	No
California	California Civil Code §704.730 (homestead); §§704.010 et seq. (personal property)	No
Colorado	Colorado Revised Statutes §§38-41-201 et seq. (homestead); §13-54-102 (personal property)	No
Connecticut	Connecticut General Statutes Annotated §52-352b (personal property)	Yes
Delaware	Delaware Code Annotated Title 10 §§4902 et seq. (personal property)	No
District of Columbia	D.C.Code Annotated §15-501 (personal property)	Yes
Florida	Florida Const. Art. X§4 (homestead/personal property); Florida Statutes §§222.11 et seq. (miscellaneous)	No
Georgia	Georgia Code Annotated §§44-13-1 et seq. (real/personal property); §44-13-100 (another option)	No

STATE	STATUTE	FEDERAL BANKRUPTCY CODE EXEMPTIONS ALLOWED
Hawaii	Hawaii Revised Statutes §651-92 (homestead); §651-121 (personal property)	Yes
Idaho	Idaho Code §§55-1001 et seq. (homestead); §§11-603 et seq. (personal property)	No
Illinois	Illinois Annotated Statutes Chapter 110 §§12-901 et seq. (homestead); §§12-1001 et seq. (personal property)	No
Indiana	Indiana Code Annotated §34-2-28-1 (real/personal property)	No
Iowa	Iowa Code Annotated §§561.1 et seq. (homestead); §§627.1 et seq. (personal property)	No
Kansas	Kansas Constitution Art. 15 §9 and Kansas Statutes Annotated §§60-2301 et seq. (homestead); §60-2304 (personal property)	No
Kentucky	Kentucky Revised Statutes Annotated §§427.060 et seq. (homestead); §§4287.010 et seq. (personal property)	No
Louisiana	Louisiana Revised Statutes Annotated §20:1 (homestead); §13:3881 (personal property)	No
Maine	Maine Revised Statutes Annotated Title 14 §4422 (homestead/personal property)	No
Maryland	Annotated Code of Maryland §11-504 (personal property)	No
Massachusetts	Massachusetts General Laws Annotated## Chapter 188 §§1 et seq. (homestead); Chapter 235 §34 (personal property)	Yes
Michigan	Michigan Constitution Article X §3 and Michigan Compiled Laws Annotated §27A.6023(h) (homestead); §600.6023 (personal property)	Yes

STATE	STATUTE	FEDERAL BANKRUPTCY CODE EXEMPTIONS ALLOWED
Minnesota	Minnesota Statutes Annotated §§510.01 et seq. (homestead); §550.37 (personal property)	Yes
Mississippi	Mississippi Code Annotated §§85-3-21 et seq. (homestead); §85-3-1 (other property)	Yes
Missouri	Missouri Annotated Statutes §§513.475 et seq. (homestead); §§513.430 et seq. (personal property)	No
Montana	Montana Code Annotated §§70-32-101 et seq. (homestead); §§25-13-608 et seq. (personal property)	No
Nebraska	Nebraska Revised Statutes §§40-101 et seq. (homestead); §§25-1552 et seq. (personal property)	No
Nevada	Nevada Constitution Art. 4 §30 and Nevada Revised Statutes Annotated §§115.005 et seq. (homestead); Nevada Constitution Art. 1 §14 and Nevada Revised Statutes Annotated §§21.090 et seq. (personal property)	No
New Hampshire	New Hampshire Revised Statutes Annotated §480:1 (homestead); §511:2 (personal property)	No
New Jersey	New Jersey Statutes Annotated §2A:17-19 (personal property)	Yes
New Mexico	New Mexico Statutes Annotated §42-10-9 (homestead); §§42-10-1 et seq. (personal property)	Yes
New York	New York Civil Practice Law and Rules §5206 (homestead); §5205 (personal property); Debtor and Creditor Law §282 et seq. (bankruptcy exemptions)	No

STATE	STATUTE	FEDERAL BANKRUPTCY CODE EXEMPTIONS ALLOWED
North Carolina	North Carolina Constitution Art. X §2 and North Carolina General Statutes §§1C-1601 et seq. (homestead); North Carolina Constitution Art. X §1 and North Carolina General Statutes §1C-1601 (personal property)	No
North Dakota	North Dakota Cent. Code §§47-18-01 et seq. (homestead); §§28-22-02 et seq. (personal property)	No
Ohio	Ohio Revised Code Annotated §2329.66 (homestead/personal property)	No
Oklahoma	Oklahoma Statutes Annotated Title 31 §2 (homestead); Title 31 §1 (other property)	No
Oregon	Oregon Revised Statutes §§23.240 et seq. (homestead); §23.160 (personal property)	No
Pennsylvania	23 Pennsylvania Cons. Statutes Annotated 42 §8124 (personal property); 42 §8123 (general monetary)	Yes
Rhode Island	Rhode Island General Laws §9-26-4 (personal property)	Yes
South Carolina	South Carolina Code Annotated §15-41-30(1) (homestead); §15-42-30 (personal property)	No
South Dakota	South Dakota Codified Laws Annotated §43-45-3 and §§43-31-1 et seq. (homestead); §§43-45-1 et seq. (personal property)	No
Tennessee	Tennessee State Constitution Art. XI §11 and Tennessee Code Annotated §§26-2-301 et seq. (homestead); §§26-2-102 et seq. (personal property)	No
Texas	Texas Codes Annotated §§41.001 et seq. (homestead); §§42.001 et seq. (personal property)	Yes

STATE	STATUTE	FEDERAL BANKRUPTCY CODE EXEMPTIONS ALLOWED
Utah	Utah Constitution Art. XXII §1 and Utah Code Annotated §§78-23-3 et seq. (homestead); §§78-23-5 et seq. (personal property)	No
Vermont	Vermont Statutes Annotated Title 27 §§101 et seq. (homestead); Title 27 §2740 (personal property)	Yes
Virginia	Virginia Code Annotated §§34-4 et seq. (homestead); §34-26 (personal property)	No
Washington	Washington Revised Code Annotated §§6.13.010 et seq. (homestead); §6.15.010 (personal property)	Yes
West Virginia	West Virginia Code §§38-9-1 et seq. (homestead); §§38-8-1 et seq. (personal property); 38-10-4 (bankruptcy exemptions)	No
Wisconsin	Wisconsin Statutes Annotated §815.20 and §990.01(14) (homestead); §815.18 (personal property)	Yes
Wyoming	Wyoming Constitution Art. 19 §9 and Wyoming Statutes Annotated §§1-20-101 et seq. (homestead); §§1-20-105 et seq. (personal property)	No

GLOSSARY

GLOSSARY

Accord and Satisfaction - Accord and satisfaction refers to the payment of money, or other thing of value, which is usually less than the amount owed or demanded, in exchange for extinguishment of the debt.

Accrue - To occur or come into existence.

Administrative Claim - A claim which takes priority in payment over any pre-petition claims in a pending bankruptcy case.

Adversary - Opponent or litigant in a legal controversy or litigation.

Adversary Proceeding - A special proceeding involving a real controversy contested by two opposing parties within a pending bankruptcy case.

Alleged Debtor - The name designated an individual against whom his or her creditors bring an involuntary bankruptcy petition.

Amortization - The process of satisfying a debt by making a series of equal payments of interest and principal over a period of time.

Appeal - Resort to a higher court for the purpose of obtaining a review of a lower court decision.

Appearance - To come into court, personally or through an attorney, after being summoned.

Appellate Court - A court having jurisdiction to review the law as applied to a prior determination of the same case.

Appraisal - An opinion concerning the value of a piece of property.

Arrears - Payments which are due but not yet paid.

Asset - The entirety of a person's property, either real or personal.

Assignee - An assignee is a person to whom an assignment is made, also known as a grantee.

Assignment - An assignment is the transfer of an interest in a right or property from one party to another.

Automatic Stay - A judicial order issued upon the filing of a bankruptcy petition which suspends legal action against the debtor until further court order lifts the stay.

Bad Faith - A willful failure to comply with one's statutory or contractual obligations.

Bad Title - A title which is not legally sufficient to transfer property to the purchaser.

Bankrupt - The state or condition of one who is unable to pay his debts as they are, or become, due.

Bankruptcy - The legal process governed by federal law designed to assist the debtor in a new financial start while insuring fairness among creditors.

Bankruptcy Code - Refers to the Bankruptcy Act of 1978, the federal law which governs bankruptcy actions.

Bankruptcy Court - The forum in which most bankruptcy proceedings are conducted.

Bankruptcy Judge - The judge appointed by the federal court of appeals to preside over bankruptcy matters.

Bankruptcy Trustee - The person, appointed by the bankruptcy judge or selected by the creditors, who takes legal title to the property of the debtor and holds it "in trust" for equitable distribution among the creditors.

Bench - The court and the judges composing the court collectively.

Bona Fide Purchaser - One who pays valuable consideration for a purchase.

Breach of Duty - In a general sense, any violation or omission of a legal or moral duty.

Burden of Proof - The duty of a party to substantiate an allegation or issue to convince the trier of fact as to the truth of their claim.

Chapter 7 - That section of the Bankruptcy Code which involves the liquidation of the debtor's estate to satisfy his or her debts.

Chapter 11 - That section of the Bankruptcy Code which involves the reorganization of the debtor's financial affairs. Relief under this section is generally available only to businesses or individuals who have interests which exceed the limits set forth under Chapter 13.

Chapter 12 - That section of the Bankruptcy Code applicable to farmers which involves the reorganization of their financial affairs.

Chapter 13 - That section of the Bankruptcy Code applicable to debtors with regular incomes which involves the reorganization of their financial affairs.

Chattel - Any tangible, movable piece of personal property as opposed to real property.

Collateral - Property which is pledged as additional security for a debt, such as a loan.

Commingle - To combine funds or property into a common fund.

Commingling of Funds - The act of mixing a client's funds with that of a fiduciary, trustee or lawyer's own funds.

Community Property - A form of ownership in a minority of states where a husband and wife are deemed to own property in common, including earnings, each owning an undivided one-half interest in the property.

Compromise and Settlement - An arrangement arrived at, either in court or out of court, for settling a dispute upon what appears to the parties to be equitable terms.

Confession of Judgment - An admission of a debt by the debtor which may be entered as a judgment without the necessity of a formal legal proceeding.

Confirmation - Judicial approval of the bankrupt's proposed plan.

Consent Judgment - An agreement reached by the parties and entered on the record with judicial approval with the same effect as a judgment.

Consumer Debt - Debts incurred by an individual for personal, family or household purposes.

Conversion - The process by which the court, the debtor, or a creditor in a bankruptcy case pending under one chapter transfers the case to another chapter.

Court - The branch of government responsible for the resolution of disputes arising under the laws of the government.

Credit - Credit is that which is extended to the buyer or borrower on the seller or lender's belief that that which is given will be repaid.

Creditor - The person or entity to whom the debtor owes a debt.

Debtor - The name designated the individual who seeks relief from his or her debts in a pending bankruptcy case.

Deed - A legal instrument conveying title to real property.

Default - Default is a failure to discharge a duty or do that which ought to be done.

Discharge - A court order which eliminates certain debts owed by the debtor for which the creditor may no longer seek payment.

Dischargeability - The status of whether a claim qualifies for discharge.

Dismissal - The termination of a pending bankruptcy case.

Docket - A list of cases on the court's calendar.

Earned Income - Income which is gained through one's labor and services, as opposed to investment income.

Escrow - The arrangement for holding instruments or money which is not to be released until certain specified conditions are met.

Estate - The entirety of the debtor's property, real or personal.

Executory Contract - An executory contract is one which has not yet been fully completed or performed at the time the debtor files a bankruptcy petition.

Exemptions - Specified items which are not property of the debtor's estate under applicable state or federal laws.

Fact Finder - In a judicial or administrative proceeding, the person, or group of persons, that has the responsibility of determining the acts relevant to decide a controversy.

Fact Finding - A process by which parties present their evidence and make their arguments to a neutral person, who issues a nonbinding report based on the findings, which usually contains a recommendation for settlement.

Fiduciary - A fiduciary is a person having a legal duty, created by an undertaking, to act primarily for the benefit of another in matters connected with the undertaking.

Filing Fee - The amount charged by the bankruptcy court for filing a bankruptcy petition.

Finance Charge - Any charge for an extension of credit, such as interest.

Finding - Decisions made by the court on issues of fact or law.

Fixed Income - Income which is unchangeable.

Fixture - Chattel which has become permanently and physically attached to real property, and which would not be easily removed.

Fraud - A false representation of a matter of fact, whether by words or by conduct, by false or misleading allegations, or by concealment of that which should have been disclosed, which deceives and is intended to deceive another, and thereby causes injury to that person.

Fraudulent Conveyance - The transfer of property for the purpose of delaying or defrauding creditors.

Garnish - To attach the wages or property of an individual.

Garnishee - A person who receives notice to hold the assets of another, which are in his or her possession, until such time as a court orders the disposition of the property.

Hearing - A proceeding to determine an issue of fact based on the evidence presented.

Homestead - The house, outbuilding, and land owned and used as a dwelling by the head of the family.

In Formal Pauperis - Latin for "in the manner of a pauper." It refers to the right of a party to proceed with a lawsuit without costs or certain formalities.

Insolvent - The status of having debts which exceed one's assets.

Installment Contract - An installment contract is one in which the obligation, such as the payment of money, is divided into a series of successive performances over a period of time.

Interest - An amount of money paid by a borrower to a lender for the use of the lender's money.

Involuntary Petition - A petition filed by an individual's creditors attempting to force him or her into bankruptcy.

Joint Tenancy - The ownership of property by two or more persons who each have an undivided interest in the whole property, with the right of survivorship, whereby upon the death of one joint tenant, the remaining joint tenants assume ownership.

Judge - The individual who presides over a court, and whose function it is to determine controversies.

Judgment - A judgment is a final determination by a court that an obligation, e.g., a sum of money, is owed by one party to another party.

Judgment Creditor - A creditor who has obtained a judgment against a debtor, which judgment may be enforced to obtain payment of the amount due.

Judgment Debtor - An individual who owes a sum of money, and against whom a judgment has been awarded for that debt.

Judgment Proof - Refers to the status of an individual who does not have the financial resources or assets necessary to satisfy a judgment.

Jurisdiction - The power to hear and determine a case.

Levy - To seize property in order to satisfy a judgment.

Lien - A claim against the property of another as security for a debt.

Loan Principal - The loan principal is the amount of the debt not including interest or any other additions.

Marital Property - Property purchased by persons while married to each other.

Maturity Date - The date upon which a creditor is designated to receive payment of a debt, such as payment of the principal value of a bond to a bondholder by the issuing company or governmental entity.

Mortgage - A written instrument, duly executed and delivered, that creates a lien upon real estate as security for the payment of a specific debt.

Motion - An application to the court requesting an order or ruling in favor of the applicant.

Natural Person - A human being as opposed to an artificial "person" such as a corporation.

Negotiable Instrument - A signed writing which contains an unconditional promise to pay a sum of money, either on demand or at a specified time, payable to the order of the bearer.

Net Worth - The difference between one's assets and liabilities.

Note - A writing which promises payment of a debt.

Obligee - An obligee is one who is entitled to receive a sum of money or performance from the obligor.

Obligor - An obligor is one who promises to perform or pay a sum of money under a contract.

Paramount Title - Refers to title which is superior over any other claim of title.

Parties - The disputants.

Partition - A division of real property among co-owners.

Pecuniary - A term relating to monetary matters.

Personal Property - All property that is not real property.

Petition - The document filed with the bankruptcy court which begins the bankruptcy case.

Petitioner - One who files a petition with the bankruptcy court..

Plan - A document filed by the debtor which sets forth the debtor's proposal to pay his or her debts over a period of time.

Preference - A transfer made within the preference period by a debtor to a creditor on account of a debt owed, that gives the creditor more than would have been received in the bankruptcy case.

Pre-petition - Occurrences which take place before a petition is filed in bankruptcy court.

Priority Claim - A claim which takes priority in payment over the claims of other creditors in a pending bankruptcy case, e.g. claims by taxing authorities.

Property of the Estate - The debtor's assets, less exemptions, which are under the control of the bankruptcy trustee.

Reaffirmation - An agreement to make payments on a debt in order to keep certain property.

Real Property - Land, and generally whatever is erected or growing upon or affixed to the land.

Referee - An individual who is appointed by the court for a specific issue and empowered to determine issues of fact for the purpose of reporting to the court concerning the particular issue so that the court can render a judgment.

Referee's Deed - A deed given by a referee or other public officer pursuant to a court order for the sale of property.

Relief - The remedies afforded a complainant by the court.

Remedy - Refers to the means by which a right is enforced or a violation of a right is compensated.

Rescission - The cancellation of a contract which returns the parties to the positions they were in before the contract was made.

Satisfaction - The discharge and release of an obligation.

Schedules - Official bankruptcy forms which set forth the debtor's debts, assets and exemptions.

Section 341 Meeting - A meeting scheduled by the Bankruptcy Court during which the debtor answers, under oath, certain questions put forth by the trustee and creditors.

Seised - The status of lawfully owning and possessing real property.

Separate Property - Property owned by a married person in his or her own right during marriage.

Settlement - An agreement by the parties to a dispute on a resolution of the claims, usually requiring some mutual action, such as payment of money in consideration of a release of claims.

Statute of Limitations - Any law which fixes the time within which parties must take judicial action to enforce rights or thereafter be barred from enforcing them.

Stipulation - An admission or agreement made by parties to a lawsuit concerning the pending matter.

Tangible Property - Property which is capable of being possessed, whether real or personal.

Tax - A sum of money assessed upon one's income, property and purchases, for the purpose of supporting the government.

Trial - The judicial procedure whereby disputes are determined based on the presentation of issues of law and fact. Issues of fact are decided by the trier of fact, either the judge or jury, and issues of law are decided by the judge.

U.S. Trustee - The representative of the U.S. Department of Justice who oversees bankruptcy cases and appoints trustees to administer the property of the bankruptcy estate.

Voidable - Capable of being rendered void and unenforceable.

BIBLIOGRAPHY